From Literature Circles to Blogs

Activities for engaging professional learning communities

SUSAN CHURCH

MARGARET SWAIN

Pembroke Publishers Limited

Acknowledgments

With thanks to Nancy, our technology guru, and to all the graduate students who encouraged us to write this book.

© 2009 Pembroke Publishers
538 Hood Road
Markham, Ontario, Canada L3R 3K9
www.pembrokepublishers.com

Distributed in the U.S. by Stenhouse Publishers
480 Congress Street
Portland, ME 04101
www.stenhouse.com

We acknowledge the financial support of the Government of Canada through the Book Publishing Industry Development Program (BPIDP) for our publishing activities.

We acknowledge the assistance of the Government of Ontario through the Ontario Media Development Corporation's Ontario Book Initiative.

Library and Archives Canada Cataloguing in Publication

Church, Susan M.

   From literature circles to blogs : activities for engaging professional learning communities / Susan Church, Margaret Swain.

Includes bibliographical references and index.
ISBN 978-1-55138-244-9

1. Elementary school teachers—In-service training. 2. Professional learning communities. I. Swain, Margaret, 1949– II. Title.

LB1731.C463 2009   370.71'55   C2009-902724-0

Editor: Jane McNulty
Cover Design: John Zehethofer
Typesetting: Jay Tee Graphics Ltd.

Printed and bound in Canada
9 8 7 6 5 4 3 2 1

Contents

Introduction

In the field of education there has never been a shortage of controversy over how we might teach more effectively so that all students learn better. Professional and scholarly publications representing a wide range of perspectives circulate in print and online. Heated debates about theories and practices play out endlessly in staff rooms and conference meeting halls.

Given this situation within the teaching profession, it is rare to find consensus coalescing around any issue, much less a highly complex one such as teacher professional development. Yet, as Darling-Hammond and Richardson (2009) reveal in a review of 20 years of research related to the topic, there is growing consensus about the need to rethink practices in professional development. Their analysis of the results of a large number of studies highlights substantive evidence that the pervasive workshop model of professional development is ineffective in creating changes in practices. As an alternative, the research supports the construction of much more powerful, sustained, collaborative, and job-embedded learning opportunities for teachers. In a synthesis of the research findings, Darling-Hammond and Richardson identify three key characteristics of effective professional development:

1. The **content** is centred on **student learning**.
2. The **context** is integrated with **school improvement**.
3. The **design** promotes **active, sustained learning**.

In the workshop model approach to professional learning, experts typically impart knowledge to teachers in one-shot sessions focused on teaching practices. In contrast, more effective professional development examines how well each teacher's students and the school population as a whole are learning and how the school can better support that learning. Teachers become actively engaged over the long term in working collaboratively with peers to improve their practices. They seek new knowledge in response to questions that they themselves generate from their continual reflection on how students are doing.

The Emergence of Professional Learning Communities

Evidence concerning the power of ongoing collaborative learning has given rise to a highly effective professional learning community model across North America. In such communities, teachers meet regularly at the worksite to inquire into how well their practices support student achievement. In the words of Darling-Hammond and Richardson (2009), teachers involved in professional learning communities "learn about, try out, and reflect on new practices in their specific context, sharing their individual knowledge and expertise." (p. 49). For example, they might read and discuss professional literature in study groups, observe one another's teaching practices, and/or examine student work together.

The shift from traditional professional development models that feature one-shot workshops or lectures from experts to an on-site collaborative approach necessitates significant changes in a school's established organizational structures and processes. Within a traditional model, teachers typically work in isolation from each other, devoting the majority of their time and effort to their interactions with students. In such a model, professional development is an event that occurs periodically. Within a professional learning community model, however, teachers must open their classroom doors and be willing and prepared to reflect critically and continuously upon their practices. The schools in which they work must find ways to provide time for teachers to learn together and they must support that learning through access to human and material resources.

Because productive collaborative work does not happen simply because teachers meet to discuss practices, school leaders must take steps to facilitate community building. This is often a complex process, especially in schools in which teachers have had little experience with collaboration. Community building requires the construction of group norms, the establishment of trust among members, and the development of ways to resolve the conflicts that will inevitably arise from time to time.

The Southwest Educational Development Laboratory, a non-profit research and development organization, reports that the research is quite clear about what successful professional learning communities look like and act like. The factors and organizational arrangements that lead to viable professional development communities include the following:

- the collegial participation of the principal, who shares leadership—and thus power and authority—by inviting staff input in decision making
- a shared vision that develops from the staff's unswerving commitment to students' learning and that is consistently articulated and referenced in relationship to the staff's work
- collective learning among staff and application of that learning to solutions that address students' needs
- the observation and review of each teacher's classroom behavior by peers as a feedback and assistance activity to support individual and community improvement
- physical conditions and human capacities that support professional development community building

The Challenges of Implementing Professional Learning Communities

Today, many schools and school districts are taking up the challenge of implementing professional learning communities. At worksites where reformers acknowledge the complexities of implementation and collaborate with teachers to construct supportive processes and structures, the positive potential of the

There is broad, even remarkable, concurrence among members of the research community on the effects of carefully structured learning teams on the improvement of instruction. Add to this that such structures are probably the most practical, affordable, and professionally dignified route to better instruction in our schools.
Schmoker, 2004, p. 430

new model is increasingly evident. However, in situations where these complex changes are mandated externally without sufficient support and within unrealistic time frames, the outcomes are, understandably, less positive.

Former school administrator Richard DuFour pioneered the development of a professional learning community in his high school, and he now devotes his time to writing and providing professional development to assist others in emulating the processes that he developed. He consistently voices concern that implementation snags will lead to the abandonment of this promising trend in school reform. He also argues that many structures—grade-level teaching teams, school committees, high school departments, school districts as a whole, and professional organizations—are erroneously labeled "professional learning communities." DuFour comments that "the term [professional learning community] has been used so ubiquitously that it is in danger of losing all meaning" (Dufour, 2007, p. 6). He urges teachers and administrators to reflect critically on what it really means to function as a professional learning community, identifying core principles or "big ideas" that schools must keep in the forefront; these core principles are summarized as follows:

1. School staffs must take seriously their responsibilities to ensure that all students learn, using three key questions to guide their work:
   • What do we want each student to learn?
   • How will we know when each student has learned it?
   • How will we respond when a student experiences difficulty in learning? (DuFour, 2004, p. 7)
2. School staffs must work to develop a culture of collaboration that moves beyond collegiality to consider issues and questions openly and to seek ways to improve practices.
3. School staffs must focus on results in terms of student learning. They should use a wide array of data to assess each student's achievement, asking, "What evidence do we have of the progress that we have made on the learning goals that we and our students set?"

Addressing Teachers' Questions and Concerns

As educators who have had long careers in public education, we are aware that professional learning communities have tremendous potential to enhance both teacher and student learning. When we fulfilled leadership roles at the school and district levels, both of us fostered opportunities for collaborative learning in our work with teachers and administrators and we know that collaborative contexts promote positive change. Today, in our interactions with teachers and administrators in our roles as instructors of university graduate courses, we hear the success stories, but we also hear about significant growing pains in many schools. The teachers' reflections on their experiences mirror the issues documented in the research literature. If they find themselves on the receiving end of external professional development mandates from the district or school administration and if they lack appropriate support, teachers

• are unclear about purposes and describe situations in which they are told when to meet, with whom to meet, and what to talk about, but they lack

direction regarding processes and structures, and they wonder, "What are we supposed to *do* in these sessions?"
- express concerns about participation in groups in which there are divergent views concerning philosophies and best practices, leading to conflicts that they have no means to resolve
- find leadership within the group problematic: Who structures each learning community session? Who makes sure materials are available? Who keeps notes? Who is the audience for the notes?
- perceive that they lack input and choice
- see the learning community sessions as simply one more obligation to add to their already overcrowded schedules
- are unable to describe changes in practices or impacts on student learning that have resulted from their participation in a professional learning community

Fortunately, many helpful articles and books offer research-based perspectives on how to avoid such frustrations. We did a quick search of an online bookstore and found 1800 entries related to professional learning communities! An Internet search yielded more than 30 million possible sites to access. In the Recommended Resources section at the back of this book, we have referenced some of the resources that we have found most helpful in addressing the issues and obstacles listed above.

So, why have we written this book? In our discussions with teachers and administrators, it became apparent that they would welcome a user-friendly resource that offers practical guidelines that teachers themselves can use to structure and sustain their collaborative learning. Teachers want to make the best use of the time set aside for professional development, focusing on student learning and their own teaching, not on the logistics of making a professional learning community succeed. Drawing on our experiences working with teachers in collaborative professional development contexts and in university graduate courses, we have compiled a wide range of ideas that teachers and administrators can adapt to suit their needs.

How This Book Is Structured

Chapter 1 provides suggestions to help educators get off on the right foot when initiating a professional learning community model, as well as activities to help participants make the transition from their work in the classroom to a context in which *they* are the learners.

Subsequent chapters focus on the specifics of how to plan and conduct professional learning community sessions.

Chapter 2 provides a range of activities in which teachers can come together to learn through reading and responding to professional resources.

Chapter 3 shows how teachers can develop a deeper understanding of the externally mandated parameters (policies, curriculum guides, and accountability frameworks) within which they work. We are aware that the terminology associated with accountability frameworks varies across provinces and states. For the sake of consistency, therefore, we have referred to accountability frameworks as "standards/outcomes" throughout this book.

Chapter 4 describes a variety of ways in which teachers can examine student work together and use insights gained through their analysis to guide planning, instruction, and assessment.

Chapter 5 describes how teachers can look critically at teaching practices by examining sample lesson plans and demonstration lessons, visiting each other's classrooms, and designing and teaching lessons together.

Chapter 6 suggests various ways in which teachers can design and implement long-term collaborations such as joint planning, co-teaching, and action research.

Chapter 7 features several scenarios showing ways in which teachers can use the activities described in the other chapters flexibly in response to specific interests and needs. For example, a group might begin by examining student work together and then decide that they need to scrutinize certain outcomes/standards more closely to see how their students' work corresponds with external expectations. They might then decide to read some professional literature, view video resources, or connect to a blog related to the curricular area on which they are focused (for example, student writing, mathematical problem solving, science inquiry, and so on).

Recognizing that collaborative work that leads to changes in practices requires trust and the exchange of honest feedback, we designed the chapters to move from activities that are less personal and less risky (engaging with print and non-print professional resources) to those that are feasible only among professionals who have developed effective working relationships and a high level of faith in each other (as evidenced by team planning and teaching). The activities themselves are designed to build trust and rapport and to expand the group's repertoire of options for self-directed learning.

In each chapter, we have included suggestions for using digital technologies to enhance learning and to extend collaboration beyond the school. We acknowledge that there is great variation across schools in terms of access to digital resources. Nevertheless, today's world is an increasingly wired one in which our students function effortlessly. Furthermore, it is an undeniable trend that more and more learning opportunities for students and teachers are becoming available online. Therefore, we determined that it was important to include some digital possibilities for professional learning communities to explore. At the same time, while our suggestions for using technology can certainly enrich learning, a professional learning community can take advantage of all of the activities in on-site, face-to-face settings if they lack access to technology or choose not to use it.

We hope that teachers and administrators will find our suggestions practical and helpful as they learn within professional learning communities in their schools and other settings. We have used versions of these activities in our work with teachers in the context of professional development sessions and university courses. Many of the activities can be adapted to the classroom, providing stimulating ways to engage students actively in their learning. We can guarantee that these are sound and well-tested approaches. We invite readers to mix, match, and adapt our ideas as they apply them thoughtfully, critically, and collaboratively.

CHAPTER 1

Activating Collaborative Learning

Life in schools is incredibly busy. The work days of both teachers and administrators are filled with interactions with students, parents/guardians, and other professionals. Teachers' work is intense. Once they hit the ground running each morning, they are in high-gear teaching mode, doing their best to respond to the needs of a diverse range of learners and to meet institutional expectations while continually negotiating relationships with administrators, peers, and parents. In the classroom, teachers typically work in isolation, with the exception of administrator visits for supervisory purposes or the presence of teachers' aides, resource teachers, or other support personnel. How, then, do school staffs make the shift from this "school business as usual" culture to a culture of collaborative professional learning?

The Key Role of School Principals

As documented in the research cited in the Introduction to this book, principals play a key role in initiating and sustaining professional learning communities within schools. To be effective, they must attach a high priority to teacher professional development and take action to foster a culture that supports collaboration.

> Educational leadership is about how leaders mobilize others to get extraordinary things done on behalf of the students we reach and teach.
> Spence, 2009, p. 7

Setting Clear Expectations

The principal's strong advocacy and enthusiastic promotion of collaborative professional learning sends a powerful message to teachers about what is fundamentally important in their daily endeavors. Principals need to express their deep commitment to student learning and their confidence that teachers have the collective expertise to address the needs of all students. Furthermore, they need to show that they believe that working together will enhance everyone's effectiveness and they need to make clear that working in isolation is not an option. Principals can also share research that demonstrates the benefits that teachers will experience through collaborative learning with peers. These benefits include the development of shared responsibility for student learning, a better understanding of how they can help students to succeed, peer assistance and support, and ongoing professional renewal.

Principals can share information related to collaborative learning in the following ways:

- Choose a short article, staple a comment sheet to the front of it, and circulate the article among staff members, inviting them to read it and write a brief response to it. Principals can encourage teachers to find and circulate articles in a similar way.

- Set up an online space (perhaps in a restricted area of the school's website) that is devoted exclusively to professional learning communities, in which teachers can interact with administrators and with each other and to which short articles, research reports, and helpful links can be posted.
- Set aside time during each staff meeting for discussion and sharing of information about professional learning communities. Possible approaches include presenting evidence from research and considering the implications for the school, highlighting the activities of one or more of the professional learning community groups already established within the school, and addressing specific issues and concerns that may have arisen as teachers begin to work together.
- Adapt any of the activities related to professional reading described in Chapter 2.

Multi-level Engagement in Setting Goals

Principals can also help to set clear expectations by engaging their school communities in planning processes that lead to a shared vision for the school and to the generation of priorities for student learning. Such collaborative goal setting provides a sound basis from which smaller professional learning communities can evolve within the school, as they focus their inquiries on specific ways to progress toward the agreed-upon goals.

Once formed, the smaller groups can engage in similar processes of setting goals for their work together. Individual teachers can steer the process toward even greater specificity through goal setting related to their own professional growth.

This multi-level engagement in setting and working toward goals creates a stronger focus and a greater coherence in the school's efforts to ensure that all students are successful. For example, a school might identify a need to improve students' problem solving in mathematics. Small groups of teachers might form to investigate specific aspects of this issue, such as using writing to enhance problem solving, teaching the language of mathematics, or improving classroom assessment of problem solving. An individual teacher in one group might develop a professional growth goal focused on using reflective questions to frame students' writing about mathematics in a Grade 5 classroom.

Small-Group Formation Within Professional Learning Communities

There is a far greater likelihood that teachers will engage productively in collaborative professional learning if they can participate in decisions regarding their involvement. The principal can encourage buy-in by allowing some choice concerning the composition and the focus of small groups. Teachers who have shared interests appreciate the opportunity to explore questions together and they will establish trust and rapport with each other more quickly as a result. They will be more likely to take their inquiries beyond talk and to make actual positive changes in their practices. While professional learning community groups often form around common grade levels or subject areas, principals and teachers should consider a range of alternatives, such as cross-curricular, cross-grade-level, or cross-school groupings, as well as online groups.

As long as the participants share an interest in a particular area of inquiry, these types of small group collaborations create opportunities for teachers to investigate a topic from different perspectives and to learn from the diverse experiences of other group members.

Modeling a Collaborative Approach

When principals themselves are collaborative in their dealings with staff, they provide models for structuring productive relationships within the school. Some collaborative practices demonstrated by principals include:

- inviting input from teachers
- listening and acting upon teachers' concerns and suggestions
- inviting alternative points of view
- engaging in group problem solving
- managing conflict in ways that protect relationships
- providing help and support in response to teachers' individual needs
- offering and accepting constructive criticism and advice
- initiating and sustaining conversations about learning and teaching
- acknowledging the contributions of staff members and expressing thanks through oral and written communication

Principals who consistently work collaboratively themselves help to build trust within the school—trust that is so essential to the success of professional learning communities. Teachers will not open their classroom doors and reveal their teaching practices or express their needs and worries honestly if they fear reprisals from the administration or from their peers.

Facilitating and Supporting Professional Learning Communities

In the beginning stages of establishing a professional learning community, the principal may need to play an active teaching role or tap into the expertise of other professionals to help groups of teachers develop the skills they will need to become self-governing. Sometimes teachers from within the groups can play this leadership role. Issues that must be addressed so that groups can function successfully include:

- Norms: attendance, punctuality, confidentiality, task focus
- Communication skills: listening, taking turns speaking, showing respect for others, demonstrating openness, accepting diverse views
- Modes of interaction for different purposes: for example, dialogue that enables members to share different perspectives and discussion that leads to consensus

- Decision making, for example, determining when to use consensus building or when to use voting
- Conflict resolution

Many of the activities suggested in this book provide frameworks for interactions that can support the development of the skills needed for collaborative learning. By engaging in the activities and then debriefing after each session, teachers will learn by doing. As they debrief, individual teachers and groups as a whole can identify areas in which they might require the assistance of the principal or another outside facilitator. Professional development related to communication, conflict resolution, decision making, or other topics can then be structured in response to teachers' identified needs. (See the Recommended Resources at the back of this book for practical references related to professional learning communities.)

Making Collaborative Learning Possible

As managers of the school's resources, principals are in the best position to address practical issues associated with on-site professional learning.

Scheduling time to meet is consistently identified as one of the most problematic aspects of implementing professional learning communities. Research shows that extended blocks of time during the school day are the most productive way to ensure meaningful learning and change, but such blocks are difficult to schedule in busy schools. Once a regular time is set aside for teachers to meet, principals must preserve that time for that purpose even when other pressing matters arise. Inventive principals have addressed this problem in a number of ways:

- Creative use of specialists and substitute teachers to allow several teachers to be freed up from the classroom at the same time
- Professional development days formerly used for workshops or other types of sessions can be reallocated to professional learning community meeting time spread over a number of half-days throughout the year
- In some districts, time is "banked" by adding extra minutes to the school day so that students receive the same amount of instruction but teachers can be freed up through regularly scheduled early dismissals. The introduction of early dismissals requires careful planning since changes in the length of the school day require adjustments to school bus schedules and may present hardships to parents in terms of childcare. Where early dismissals have been successful, schools have involved parents and guardians from the outset, helping them to understand the importance of the work done during the time set aside for professional learning. In some situations, principals have been able to arrange school- or community-based childcare or recreational programs to take place on the early dismissal afternoons.

One high school principal scheduled an assembly every two weeks that he planned and facilitated, thus freeing up teachers to meet in professional learning sessions. In order to make the assemblies purposeful learning experiences, the principal involved students in the planning and delivery of sessions for their peers. Community members were invited to the assemblies to share their perspectives and expertise. Teachers made a commitment to follow up the assemblies with lessons that made connections between the curriculum and the topics addressed during each assembly.

Providing resources is a tangible means by which principals can support professional learning. These resources include:

- professional books, articles, or websites related to a topic being explored
- computers and software for online learning and digital interactions with professional learning communities and educators beyond the school
- access to expertise from outside the school to support inquiries, for example, district consultants, literacy or math coaches, and student services personnel such as psychologists or speech therapists
- data on student achievement
- funding for memberships in professional organizations that can extend teachers' learning
- food, beverages, and consumable materials such as pencils, pens, markers, post-it notes, notebooks, and so on, to be given to participants at professional learning community meetings

Suggesting formats and structures to guide the work of professional learning communities is important, especially during the initial stages. Principals can offer ideas for how a small group of teachers interested in a particular aspect of learning can launch an inquiry into the topic and link it to student learning and to their own teaching practices. They can provide or help teachers develop protocols for activities such as examining student work and peer observation. (See Chapters 3 and 4 for examples of such protocols.)

Principals must establish regular channels of communication between the small groups and the school administration so that issues can be addressed and support provided as needed. Making professional learning communities a regular topic at staff meetings and setting up an online space for information sharing and communication can help ensure that positive accomplishments as well as problems come to the attention of the principal in a timely manner. The principal can use a simple communication form for each professional learning community to submit either as a hard copy or online on a regular basis—perhaps once a month—to keep the administration informed and connected to the groups. The sample form on page 16 includes space for the principal to write comments, thereby fostering two-way communication. (A blank version of this form is included as a blackline master at the back of this book.)

Shared Leadership

While principals play vital roles in establishing and sustaining collaborative cultures in schools, they clearly have many other responsibilities. Furthermore, administrators bring different strengths and aptitudes to their roles. Some have strong interpersonal skills and the ability to foster staff engagement and commitment to working together and, thus, may choose to take a direct and active part in leading professional learning community activities in the school. In other situations, however, the principal may not be the best person to take on this responsibility, based on his or her leadership style or the demands of other

Principal's Communication Form: Professional Learning Communities

This form is intended to keep me informed regarding the work of the professional learning communities in the school so that I can support them in every way possible. I will return this form to you with my comments before your next meeting. Please fill in and submit this form each month, updating it from the previous report as your learning evolves. Good luck!

Date: _October 2, 2009_

Group members: _Helen, Natalie, Brian, Rashida, Dennis, Tabitha_

Learning focus (please indicate if, and if so how, this focus has changed since your last report):
We've been looking at our students' writing in content areas and have seen that most of them are having trouble with organizing their ideas. We're reading articles on content writing and will be trying out some of them in our classrooms.

Meetings and activities this month:
October 1 – Brought writing to share
October 15 – Continued looking at writing
October 29 – Brought books and articles on content writing; read one together and agreed on reading to complete for next session

Highlight important insights or questions that have emerged:
- _We haven't been providing students with enough examples of effective non-fiction writing._
- _We feel overwhelmed by getting through the curriculum in science, social studies, and health, much less spending more time with writing...how do we get to everything?_

How can I support your work?
Are you aware of any Grades 4-6 teachers who are especially competent at teaching content writing?

Principal's feedback:
I'll see what I can find out re. teachers in schools in the area. How would you feel about asking the literacy coach to one of your meetings? I talked with her and she has some additional resources, including some videos. Let me know.

aspects of the principal's role. Moreover, one of the characteristics of collaborative school cultures is that leadership responsibilities are shared among staff, students, parents/guardians, and community members. Therefore, many principals choose to involve others directly in supporting and facilitating professional learning communities.

Individuals in formal leadership positions, for example, vice-principals or high school department heads, can gain valuable experience through engagement with professional learning communities. While the principal is responsible for setting expectations regarding collaborative learning in the school, these administrators can be more hands-on, facilitating small group sessions, providing resources, and interacting directly with the collaborative groups.

As groups of teachers gain experience in working together, leaders may emerge from within the groups. These teachers will have established credibility with their peers and are often eager to take on leadership roles. Some small groups develop very effective shared leadership models in which individuals take turns assuming leadership responsibilities, and the group determines how tasks can be distributed equitably among the teachers.

From time to time, it may be helpful for principals to draw upon leadership from outside the school, for example, curriculum specialists, staff developers, or other experts. Such individuals can bring fresh perspectives and insights. Furthermore, bringing someone in from outside the school may be beneficial if there are internal conflicts that the school has not been able to address satisfactorily. When the school administration and the staff are in conflict, the assistance of an external facilitator may be necessary in order to resolve the problem.

In her book *Becoming a Literacy Leader* (Stenhouse, 2006), literacy specialist Jennifer Allen provides practical suggestions for leading teacher study groups and facilitating other forms of professional development. A companion DVD *Teacher Study Groups* is also available through Stenhouse.

Leadership is undoubtedly a key issue in the success of professional learning communities. However, the participants themselves must all demonstrate commitment to active involvement in directing their own learning. The next section discusses how teachers can create contexts in which their own learning is paramount, as they progress from their complex teaching responsibilities to becoming part of a vibrant learning community.

Transition From Teacher to Learner

Even when schedules align and teachers are freed from their teaching responsibilities to focus on their own learning in collaborative groups, making the transition from the busy work day to a learning context can be challenging. Outlined on the following pages are a number of suggestions for ways to open sessions in order to facilitate this transition, as well as to build trust and rapport in the early stages of meeting together. Initially, the principal or a designated group leader will need to take responsibility for these transition activities. Once the group has become more self-directive, however, members can take turns fulfilling this leadership role.

Transition activities such as those described in this chapter should be brief (no more than five minutes), and non-threatening. They are designed to bring all participants into a positive frame of mind for learning and they should be varied and adaptable to sustain novelty and interest.

Word of the Day

Post a sheet of chart paper in the meeting area and write a word in the centre of the paper. The word can be related to a specific topic being explored (e.g., *book, comprehension, rubric, algorithm, spelling,* and so on), connected more generally to student learning (e.g., *behavior, engagement, differentiation*), or open-ended and non-specific (e.g., *why, flow, success,* and so on). Provide markers and ask participants to write or draw a response to the word or to someone else's response. Encourage the use of lines, arrows, and other graphics to show connections among words. Debrief quickly by reviewing what everyone has recorded.

Finish the Sentence

Prepare word strips with sentence starters and ask participants to complete each sentence and then post the strips around the room. The starters can be the same for everyone or there can be sets of different starters. Here are some examples:

The best thing about teaching is _____ .

The worst thing about teaching is_____ .

Today I feel_____ .

This morning I laughed about _____ .

My students are _____ .

I like to _____ .

I don't like to _____ .

Classroom Photo Montage

Take photos in classrooms and create a montage that demonstrates the many positive ways in which students are engaged in learning in the school. Invite participants to make comments on post-it notes. Give everyone an opportunity to read the comments and to talk about the photos.

Write a "Can-Do" About a Colleague

Record the names of all the participants in the professional learning community group on small slips of paper. Invite each person to draw the name of a colleague from a hat or a bag and then write and share a "can-do" (a list of three or four things that the person does well) about the person.

Surprise Packages

Occasionally, place a small wrapped gift (a pencil or pen, sticky notes with humorous illustrations or captions, a small plant, specialty tea bags, etc.) at each participant's place at the meeting table. Have recipients guess what is in the package. As an alternative, create a grab-bag of small gifts from which participants can draw as they enter the session.

Storytelling

In an article published in 2009, Bunting describes how a school established a story hour for teachers—a time when they could come together and tell stories about their work. She writes about how the story hour evolved as teachers moved from entertainment and community building to sharing personal narratives that helped them make sense of their work. For these teachers, stories

> …spoke about the cost of lost purpose, the power of reflection, and the rewards of taking responsibility for your destiny as a teacher. Stories intertwined thinking with feeling, purpose with action, and self-reliance with community. (Bunting, 2009, p. 519)

Professional learning communities can adapt this approach as an ongoing introductory activity for individual sessions or as a way to establish trust and a sense of community when teachers first begin to work together. Participants can volunteer to be the storyteller of the day, and the session can start with a story. The invitation can be open-ended so that the storyteller can choose a topic. Alternatively, volunteers can be asked to tell a story related to the topic selected as the focus of the group's current inquiry.

Practicing Mindfulness

Open the session with activities designed to divert the mind away from the distractions of a busy day through progressive relaxation, breathing exercises, visualization, or simple yoga stretches.

Artifacts

Have each participant bring in an artifact that represents something significant about them as a teacher. Artifacts can be found or hand-made. Examples might include a favorite song (recorded or performed by the participant); a poem or work of visual art (by another writer/artist or by the participant); an object; a book; a cartoon; a photograph; a plant or flower, and so on. Encourage creativity and a diverse range of representations.

Quick-Write

Post a quote from a book or an article that the group is reading. Distribute small sheets of paper or file cards and ask each participant to respond briefly to the quote in writing. Have teachers share their responses with a partner.

"Ain't It Awful!"

When school life has been particularly busy or stressful, it can be helpful to release pent-up emotions by allowing everyone a few minutes to vent about what has been difficult in their lives. These "ain't it awful!" sessions are remarkably powerful in clearing the mind so that participants can make the transition into a productive work session with a more positive focus.

Expanding the Community Through Web 2.0

With appropriate access to hardware, software, and training, professional learning communities can take advantage of digital technology in a variety of ways. In the corporate world, the shift that companies have made from selling products online to providing services online has given rise to the terminology known as "Web 2.0". In a corporate context, the term refers to services and functions that enable users to access the Internet to facilitate participation, collaboration, and distribution of information and ideas. In education and more generally, Web 2.0 refers to new ways in which learning is occurring using digital services and functions. It is now possible for a diverse range of individuals and groups to post information and opinions, to receive feedback, and to respond to each other online. The Internet allows people working at a distance from each other to collaborate to create products, play games, and share ideas. Digital networks facilitate the wide distribution of information and expertise, allowing users to create as well as access knowledge and to form interactive online communities.

Professional learning communities can greatly expand their inquiries through thoughtful use of Web 2.0 technologies. Learning to use these tools not only enhances the teachers' own professional learning but it will also provide direct experience with the new forms of literacy that students are increasingly negotiating with ease in their lives outside of school. "Literacy 2.0" is the term used to describe how "people are appropriating digital applications, networks, and services; and they are developing ways of reading, writing, viewing, listening and recording that embody this 2.0 ethos" (Knobel and Wilber, 2009, p. 21). These digital literacy practices are participatory and collaborative and they contribute to wide distribution of knowledge and expertise. Thus, they are a powerful extension of the kinds of interactions with people and texts that characterize successful face-to-face professional learning communities.

Using Web 2.0 Tools

There are wide-ranging technological tools that continue to expand as innovators find new ways to use the Internet for collaborative purposes. These tools feature both synchronous (in real time) and asynchronous (not in real time) applications. Synchronous tools include audioconferencing, web conferencing, and videoconferencing; chat rooms; instant messaging; and white boarding. Asynchronous tools include applications such as discussion boards, Web logs (blogs), wikis, email, podcasts, streaming audio, streaming video, document libraries, databases, and website links.

While synchronous communication has the advantage of spontaneity and facilitates interaction that is more akin to face-to-face communication, asynchronous tools enable people to connect at each person's convenience. These tools accommodate communication across multiple time zones as well. Such tools also allow for more reflection time, because responses can be delayed and given more thoughtful consideration. A number of Web-based platforms provide the functionality of these tools but they do so in an integrated way so that users have a single entry point for multiple forms of interaction. For example, various online learning platforms used in university and school settings allow users to post documents and links to other Web-based resources, conduct discussions synchronously and asynchronously, create forums for selected participants, and manage interactions among participants efficiently. Such platforms are being used more and more often for the delivery of online courses.

⊕⊕⊕ Web 2.0—Mini-Glossary

blog: a website, usually maintained by an individual, that facilitates regular entries (e.g., commentaries, graphics, and videos). Entries are commonly displayed in reverse chronological order. Blogger (www.blogger.com) is a free blog-hosting service.

social networking: the creation of online communities in which members exchange thoughts and comments and post photos and other visuals. Ning (www.ning.com) is a free social networking site.

wiki: a shared website that can be modified by users. A free wiki platform is available through PBworks wiki (http://pbworks.com/academic.wiki).

podcast: a series of digital computer files, usually either in audio or video format, that are released periodically and made available for download. Podomatic (www.podomatic.com) is a free hosting site for podcasts.

Ourmedia: a free hosting site for images, texts, video clips, and audio clips (www.ourmedia.org).

Professional Learning Networks

Recognizing the potential of Web 2.0 tools, providers of teacher professional development—provincial, state, and district authorities; professional organizations; and private sector consultancies—are all actively developing and promoting online learning for teachers. In particular, there is an emphasis on connecting teachers with each other and with those who have expertise in a wide range of topics of interest to teachers. For teachers who are keen to tap into broader professional learning networks, the best place to start is most likely with district or provincial/state information technology support services. The professionals working in those departments know what tools and platforms are available locally and they often initiate opportunities for teachers with similar interests to network with each other. Many provincial and state departments of education are funding innovative teacher networking projects to support educational reform.

Many organizations are instituting various types of teacher networks and creating integrated platforms to support teacher learning, for example:

- A free teacher network (http://www.teachers.tv) originating in the United Kingdom provides access to online video resources and to a variety of smaller networking groups focused on particular subject areas or topics.
- A similar network in the United States (http://www.teachersnetwork.org) run by teachers for teachers has been operating for more than two decades. Its website offers links to video and print resources, lesson plans, online conferences, and support for new teachers.
- The Canadian Network for Innovation in Education (www.cnie-rcie.ca) is open to teachers who purchase a membership for a yearly fee. This group is "a national organization of professionals committed to excellence in the

provision of innovation in education in Canada." It is a pan-Canadian, bilingual network that provides both synchronous and asynchronous learning opportunities for teachers.

- Originating in Ontario, the ABEL (Advanced Broadband Enhanced Learning) site (www.abelearn.ca) provides a range of online learning opportunities and access to professional networks.

There are also many worthwhile professional development opportunities sponsored by professional organizations, but most of these have a cost associated with them. They may be an option, however, for those who have access to funding for professional development. Often, these organizations post conference presentations or deliver workshops online. They make available video resources demonstrating current teaching practices. Members can access journals and other publications online. Many provincial and state professional organizations also offer online resources, sponsor teacher networks, and provide online learning opportunities.

Selected Professional Organizations Offering Online Learning

Because a large number of professional organizations exist, it is impossible to list them all; however, several major North American groups along with their website addresses are provided below:

Association for Supervision and Curriculum Development (ASCD)
www.ascd.org
International Reading Association (IRA) www.reading.org
National Council of Teachers of English (NCTE) www.ncte.org
National Council of Teachers of Mathematics (NCTM) www.nctm.org
National Science Teachers Association (NSTA) www.nsta.org
National Council for the Social Studies (NCSS) www.socialstudies.org
National Staff Development Council (NSDC) www.nsdc.org
Council for Exceptional Children (CEC) www.cec.sped.org
International Society for Technology in Education (ISTE) www.iste.org

---

Collaboration in a Digital Context

As we embrace the advantages that Web 2.0 offers for schools and students, let's remember that online interactions will never replace the human connections that underlie the most powerful education.
Reeves, 2009, p. 89

As noted in the Introduction to this book, access to digital technologies varies greatly from school to school. Furthermore, although most young people in schools live comfortably in a digital world—interacting through online social networks and using a wide number of applications as part of daily life—adults, including teachers, often have a much steeper learning curve when it comes to the bewildering array of digital teaching and learning options. Exploring the use of Web 2.0 tools as part of professional learning community work can help teachers become more familiar with how these tools function and to feel more confident incorporating technology in the classroom. All teachers need in order to begin is motivation, a willingness to learn, and basic technology skills. These skills include keyboarding, file management, ability to connect a camera and a microphone headset, and some experience with the Internet.

As long as the appropriate hardware and software are accessible to the members of a professional learning community, they can incorporate many applications quite seamlessly, for example, searching the Internet for relevant resources, accessing articles from a database, downloading information from a website, or interacting asynchronously with peers. These applications are simply additional ways in which the professional learning community can expand its knowledge and insights through research. When a group takes the additional step to interact synchronously with peers through audio- or videoconferencing, however, greater complexity and abstraction are added to the collaborative learning. It is important that the professional learning community members have developed trust and skill in interacting face-to-face with each other before reaching out beyond the school.

When using digital technologies for real-time collaborative learning, teachers must apply all of the same effective communication skills that they use in their on-site sessions: careful listening, turn-taking, staying on topic, and so on. While skilled facilitation is important in all discussions, it is especially crucial in online contexts. Someone needs to take on leadership tasks: logistics such as schedules, time frames and planning; facilitation of the session (introducing participants, making sure everyone has a chance to participate, keeping the discussion moving and on topic, and so on); and follow-up communication. Perhaps someone from within the professional learning community who has appropriate skills can take on this role. It might be helpful, however, if the group can tap into leadership from outside the school. Often district technology consultants are only too willing to support online teacher learning.

A professional learning community might be able to join an existing network sponsored and facilitated by the school district or by provincial or state departments of education. Consultants at that level can be very helpful in connecting school- based professional learning communities with ongoing initiatives. In most situations, expert help is available if schools seek it out.

The Collaborative Work Begins

Once professional learning communities have been formed based on members' common interests and the logistical issues of when and where to meet have been addressed, what then? While there are many possible ways for a newly established professional learning community to begin, we have found that it can be helpful to take some time to extend the participants' shared understanding of a topic that is of interest to them. Reading and discussing professional resources within a structured framework is a means through which group members can grow comfortable with each other and gain experience in working together.

Chapter 2 discusses how groups can engage actively and purposefully with texts through reading, discussion, writing, and other forms of representation. We designed the activities to be user-friendly and flexible. We suggest that groups try out a few of our suggestions and determine which approaches best meet their purposes, adapting and redesigning them as needed.

Activities to Support Professional Reading

Many educators focus their own learning through reading, responding to, and sharing their thoughts about and connections to professional materials. Most teachers find the wealth of useful and exciting materials that is currently available both encouraging and discouraging.

While many of these resources have the potential to support a teacher's work, there is so much material that getting to it all or making good choices can be overwhelming for even the most ardent reader. It is daunting to choose from the many books on every topic and from amongst every aspect of the various topics, as well as from magazine, journal, and website articles; information on chat rooms or blogs; program manuals and resource kit guidebooks; curriculum guides; and pamphlets. Additionally, ministries or departments of education, school districts, and professional associations publish and disseminate a variety of resources. Recommendations for professional reading come from administrators, colleagues, university professors, and self-directed research. There is an implicit expectation that teachers will always have the time, energy, and desire to read, reflect, learn, and find ways to integrate new insights into their work with students.

Given the masses of resources available, professional learning communities often focus initial work on collaborative professional reading. The activities described in this chapter are designed to foster readers' active engagement with texts by sharing perceptions, making classroom connections, and reflecting on how issues apply to specific classrooms. The activities support teacher participation in the exploration of any topic that is of interest to the group.

Each of the activities can also be adapted to use with learners of all ages. Some activities will be familiar to teachers from their own work with students. After using the activity for their own exploration, teachers can discuss how they might try a similar approach with their students. Members of the group may try one or more activities in the classroom and then share the results at the next professional learning community session. Suggestions and examples for classroom applications are included after each activity. (See sections titled "Into the Classroom.")

Choosing What and How to Read

Once members of a professional learning community have chosen an area of interest and have decided to explore the professional literature on that topic, they must determine how to structure their work, considering questions such as those listed on the following page.

- Will all participants read the same text (book, book chapter, or article)?
- If everyone reads the same text, will each participant read the same or different sections?
- Will participants read the material on-site and then discuss it, or will they read it on their own time and come to the session prepared for discussion?
- Will each participant read a different text on the same topic?
- If participants read different texts, will they choose their own or will it be provided?
- Will all the materials be on the same topic or will individuals or smaller groups read texts on different topics?
- Will all the readings be on the same aspect of the topic or will they address different aspects?

The activities outlined below provide various ways to structure collaborative reading. They are designed to accommodate a variety of situations and styles of working. A professional learning community can use one approach consistently or experiment with several suggestions.

Activities for Connecting With Texts

1. Literature Circles

Many teachers are familiar with literature circles as part of their classroom work with students. Daniels defines these groups as follows:

> Literature circles are small, peer-led discussion groups whose members have chosen to read the same story, poem, article, or book. While reading each group-assigned portion of the text (either in or outside of class), members make notes to help them contribute to the upcoming discussion, and everyone comes to the group with ideas to share. Each group follows a reading and meeting schedule, holding periodic discussions on the way through the book. When they finish a book, the circle members may share highlights of their reading with the wider community; then they trade members with other finishing groups, select more reading, and move into a new cycle. (Daniels, 2002, p. 2)

Like a book club, a literature circle may suit the purposes of a professional learning community by providing a framework for reading and discussion. Within a large professional learning community, several small literature circles can read different texts, thus providing opportunities for members to address areas of specific interest.

At the outset, groups may wish to use the roles that Daniels developed to help readers explore the text actively and to stay focused on their discussion. Daniels identifies four basic roles: connector, questioner, literary luminary/passage master, and illustrator. (Descriptions of these roles are included as a blackline master at the back of this book; see "Literature Circle Roles for Teacher Discussion Groups.") The role descriptions can be copied and distributed to individuals or printed and posted for reference throughout the session(s).

Every year we [the authors] engage pre-service and graduate teacher education students in literature circle discussions as an integral part of their course work. Without fail, the students tell us that it is their favorite activity.

Daniels offers a note of caution regarding the roles. These roles can certainly facilitate readers' participation in a group activity; however, if participants focus too much on the roles rather than on their engagement with the text, discussions can become stilted or mechanical.

2. QQC (Quote, Question, Comment/Connection)

In this activity, participants read the same text on their own time, respond individually on their own time, and prepare for group discussion.

- Each participant receives the text to be read and one large index card. The card limits the amount of writing that is expected. Participants read the text before the next session and use the card to record a quote from the text (this can be a quote the reader agrees or disagrees with or does not fully understand), one or two questions that arose during reading, and a personal connection, opinion, or comment about the reading. Participants bring the cards with them to the next session.
- Groups of colleagues (no more than three or four) form a group to share and discuss their quotes, their questions, and the personal connections they made to the reading.
- Several of these small groups share their responses. After all participants have discussed their reactions, each small group can share their thoughts with the larger group, outlining the issues, ideas, and questions that arose from their reading. The small group reports can be discussed further, they can lead into another activity, or they can be recorded for future reflection.

Into the Classroom

Teachers can use the QQC strategy in their classrooms, adapting it to different situations as described below.
- At the very early grade levels, young children in pairs or small groups can read aloud their favorite (or least favorite) quote from a story and then talk about their choice. Alternatively, they can read a passage and talk about how it reminds them of an experience or experiences of their own.
- Older students can record their own quotes, questions, and comments/connections in response to the reading or use the technique with informational material to record
  - something new or surprising,
  - a new question they now have about this topic, and/or
  - a personal reaction to the topic.
- Students can use this strategy when dealing with controversial materials—issues in content areas, for example—to focus discussion and to allow all students a chance to participate.

---

3. Save the Last Word for Me

Adapted from Harste, Short, and Burke (1988), this reading response activity encourages each reader to connect actively to the text and to receive and share feedback with their colleagues. The activity can be done in two ways. The text can be read on-site together or participants can read it off-site and prepare notes to bring to the next session. This activity stresses the different experiences and knowledge that each teacher brings to the text and provides opportunities for all participants to voice their impressions and questions based on the text. Since this activity can be frustrating for those participants who tend to dominate discussions (especially discussions revolving around controversial topics), it is important that the facilitator clarifies the activity procedures in advance and ensures that everyone follow the rules as outlined below.

Protocol and Procedures for On-Site Reading

- Each participant is supplied with a copy of the text (article, chapter of a book, and so on) and reads silently. The text should be reasonably brief so that it can be read in one session.
- The group or the facilitator marks in advance specific places in the text where all the readers will stop. At each of these prearranged spots, participants stop reading and go back to highlight (or jot down) a phrase, sentence, or brief passage that caught their attention. After everyone has had a chance to read the section and highlight the part they wish to share, one person reads their chosen phrase, sentence, or passage aloud. At this point the reader says nothing more. The other participants then have an opportunity to speak about what has just been read aloud. This part of the discussion can be round-robin style, with each person speaking once, or it can feature a more open give-and-take format.
- When all participants have had a chance to discuss what was read, the person who read the quote then makes a final comment about it. At that point, he or she can summarize everything that was said or add something new—but that person has the "last word."
- The next person in the group now reads their quote from that section, the group discusses it, and the reader has the final word. The process repeats itself until all participants have had an opportunity to share their quote.
- The whole group then reads the next section and repeats the process, which continues until the group has completed reading and discussing the entire text.

Protocol and Procedures for Off-Site Reading

- Participants are given a text to read on their own time and they are asked to jot down several phrases, sentences, or passages on the front of a small index card (jotting one quote per card).
- On the back of the card, they jot down notes about why they chose that quote.
- When the group gets together, each person takes a turn reading one of their quotes (indicating the page/paragraph in the text so that others can find it), listening to the responses of their colleagues within the group, and then stating their own "last word" on the quote, using both what they have written themselves and what they have heard during the discussion.
- In this procedure, it is not necessary to chunk the reading; participants can select quotes from anywhere in the text, and quotes do not need to follow the sequence in which they appear in the text.

4. Say Something

...purposeful student-to-student talk is probably the most underrepresented teaching and learning practice that we can think of.
Harvey and Goudvis, 2007, p. 53

Also adapted from Harste, Short, and Burke (1988), this on-site reading response activity for pairs or small groups allows participants to share and deepen their understanding of a text together. It highlights the social nature of language and the importance of opportunities to interact and learn along with others.

With input from the group, the facilitator introduces a question pertaining to the topic, outcome, or goal that the group is exploring together. Prior to the session, the facilitator has found and made copies of a text that addresses some aspect of the issue or question under discussion.

- Participants choose one or two reading partners (or partners are assigned by the facilitator). Each participant in the pair/group works with a copy of the text. Participants choose whether they wish to read aloud or silently. Before reading, participants (or the facilitator) choose(s) to mark several places in the text where they will stop reading and "say something."
- All participants start reading up to the first designated spot. When each person has finished reading the section, one person starts by "saying something" about what they have just read. They can summarize the section, make a personal connection to the text, or point out something with which they agreed or disagreed. A second person now has an opportunity to "say something" about what they have just read or about the comments made by the previous participant. This part of the activity can proceed on a "one person, one chance to comment" basis, or it can follow a more informal give-and-take format. After each participant has had a chance to "say something," the group reads along to the next designated spot and each participant is once again asked to "say something" about what they have just read.
- This process is repeated until the pair/group has finished reading the entire text. When all the pairs/groups have finished reading, the facilitator can focus a whole group discussion on how the text addressed the issue/topic/question that the group is exploring, asking participants to support their comments with specific quotes from the text.

5. Inkshedding

This writing activity was developed during the 1980s by Jim Reither and Russ Hunt of St. Thomas University, New Brunswick (www.stthomasu.ca/~hunt/dialogic/whatshed.htm). "Inkshedding" is a form of written conversation that offers several benefits for all participants, including the group facilitator. This activity provides a glimpse into what each participant is thinking about a specific issue at a particular moment. When responses are recorded and shared, the entire group gets to see the full range of interests or attitudes and the diversity of experience and opinions that exist within the group. The anonymity of the activity allows everyone to participate, regardless of whether or not they are comfortable speaking up in a group. In situations in which a few voices are dominating discussions, a version of inkshedding can be helpful. This activity can also highlight specific areas within the topic or issue being explored to which participants may need to focus their attention more strategically.

Inkshedding Version #1

- After reading a section of text, each participant records a passage from that section to which they would like others in the group to respond. The selected passage can be printed at the top of a sheet of paper that is then passed around for other participants to comment on. Each quote can also be written on a separate sheet of chart paper and posted so that individuals, pairs, or groups can circulate around the room, reading the quotes and writing their own responses to each one. (Note that passing around a sheet of paper allows for anonymity and may be preferable when groups are in an early stage of working together.)
- When everyone has had an opportunity to read the quote and write a comment of their own, the participant who chose the quote takes back the sheet of paper, reads over all the comments, thinks about their own position on an issue, and then shares ideas with the group as a whole.

Inkshedding Version #2

- At the end of a shared experience such as discussing a text, viewing a video or a presentation, or reading an article together, the group facilitator asks all participants to do a five-minute "free-write." It is important

Perhaps the most interesting effect of inkshedding is its ability to reveal diversity in the classroom. Teachers know from their perspective that what works for one student often does not work for others, but students often generalize from the experience of one.
Wyche-Smith, S. (see Bibliography, p. 112)

that participants realize that "free-writes" are to be done quickly and anonymously.

For example, participants might respond to the following question: "Given the article we just read, how do you think our school might proceed in promoting greater parent/guardian involvement in literacy goals?"

- Free-writes can also focus on the group's overall goal. Participants can respond to the following types of questions at the beginning of or midway through the series of sessions:
  - What are your specific interests in this goal related to building a professional learning community?
  - Where are you now in your understanding or implementation of this goal?
  - How do you feel about the effectiveness of these sessions?

- Upon completion, the free-writes are handed in to the facilitator, who reads through all the responses after the session, highlighting interesting sections to be either read aloud, recorded in print form, or displayed on an overhead or whiteboard to be shared anonymously at the next session. These responses then become starting points for discussion at that session.

Into the Classroom

- In small groups, students can read a text and jot down a quote (or a favorite sentence or passage) on a sheet of paper, underline it, and then pass it around so that each other person in the group can respond to the quote in writing. Finally, each sheet of paper is passed back to the person who chose the quote. After reviewing the comments, the student can read their quote aloud and add their own comments, incorporating ideas from the group as well as their own.

- Before students read informational text, the teacher can post several quotes/passages in the classroom and have students write or offer oral comments about them. These comments are recorded in writing along with any questions students might have. Students can then read and discuss the entire text and, when appropriate, refer back to comments they made before reading the text to see how their ideas have changed.

- When given a topic or a question in a content area (for example, science, social studies, art, or health), students can do a five-minute free-write and hand their writing in to the teacher. The teacher chooses portions of these free-writes to share anonymously with the class at a later session, thus demonstrating different understandings, viewpoints, interpretations, and opinions. Having engaged the students personally yet anonymously with a particular topic or issue, the teacher can follow up this activity with a related activity or further reading.

- Teachers working in higher grades can ask students to do a free-write about the course or unit so far, encouraging students to jot ideas about what they do or do not understand, about what they like or dislike about a text, and/or about what questions they would like answered. Once again, anonymity allows students to be honest and allows teachers to receive valuable information about students' level of comprehension and engagement with content.

6. Jigsaw

When undertaken by a group of teachers, this tried-and-true cooperative learning strategy can strengthen a professional learning community. Each member is responsible for one aspect of the learning and each aspect is essential to full understanding on the part of the group as a whole. Therefore, each participant's role is essential to the entire group's learning experience. Because each participant becomes an "expert" in one area, the entire group achieves a much greater depth of understanding of material than if each member were responsible for the entire text. This strategy also allows the group to engage with a large amount of text material in an efficient manner—which is always an important factor for busy teachers. The jigsaw strategy proceeds as follows:

1. The facilitator divides a text into parts. The text can be a long article or book chapter divided into sections, or a book divided into chapters or subsections. If necessary, larger groups can be split off into smaller "home groups" comprising the same number of participants as sections of text.
2. Each participant in a small home group gets a copy of a portion of the text that they will each read and present.
3. Participants read their part of the text and make notes. (This step may be done either on-site or off-site in preparation for the next session.)
4. If there are several small groups, the participants get together in "expert groups" in which each member has read the same section of text. This group discusses what they have read, shares their notes and observations, and talks about the most effective way to present that section of text to the rest of their home group.
5. The home groups reassemble and each participant shares a summary of their section of the text as well as their interpretations, connections, and opinions related to that section.

Into the Classroom

Jigsaw is a useful cooperative learning strategy to use with students of all ages. It gives students a sense of the importance of their specific role and responsibility in relationship to both the home group and the expert group. As well, when they meet in expert groups, students share ideas with and learn from others who are doing the same task.

- When completing an inquiry project, each student in a group can take responsibility for researching and reporting on a different subtopic. For example, if groups are researching and preparing presentations on animals (local, endangered, favorite, jungle, and so on) the whole group can decide on specific categories of information such as *description, habitat, position in a food chain (what it eats and what eats it), social groupings, interactions with humans,* and so on. Students can work in home groups of five (or according to the number of categories of information) and each group can choose a different animal to investigate. Within the home group, each member then researches a topic in a different category for the chosen animal. Expert groups comprised of all the students researching a specific category, such as *habitat,* meet to talk about the kind of information to research, possible sources of information, and the most effective ways to present the information. Then the home groups come together, and each member shares information related to a different aspect of the same animal. Finally, each home group makes a brief presentation of their findings to the class. This process can be adapted to any topic in any subject area: countries, sports, diseases, hazardous chemicals, historical events, scientific discoveries, and so on.

- A jigsaw structure can also be used to gather information on a single topic, with group members choosing different resources to use in their research: informational books, magazines, fictional stories, websites, and primary sources (for example, interviews).

- Very young students especially enjoy jigsaw activities. For example, when studying colors in the environment, each home group can be assigned a specific color. Within each group, each student can look for items of that color in a different location (in the classroom, on the playground, at home, in the park, and so on.) Each group can then share and represent their color as it appeared in many different places.

- The jigsaw activity can also be used in productive ways during language arts classes. Within a small home group, each student can choose a different text (book, chapter, article, blog, and so on) for which a specific topic to explore has been assigned. For example, a group of young students can read and discuss the role of the wolf, the witch, princes, or cats in various stories. In older grades, topics can be more sophisticated. Within a small home group, each reader explores a different text but focuses on a single topic or aspect of a topic. Readers can be at very different levels of reading ability yet still contribute to the whole group's understanding of a topic.

7. Read and Present

While similar to the jigsaw activity, "Read and Present" asks individual participants to go beyond simply sharing comments or notes and to take responsibility for ensuring that others in the group *learn* important aspects of a specific text, topic, or issue. In this activity, each participant not only shares the content of the material but also demonstrates their expertise in teaching and learning. For example, a group might investigate a series of books or articles on different aspects of a topic, such as using graphic organizers in the Grade 4 classroom, reading in the content areas, teaching poetry in high school, developing students' independent use of mathematical problem-solving strategies, engaging middle school students in inquiry, and so on. A high level of trust and comfort within the group is required before teachers can be open to teaching each other and receiving feedback from peers.

- The facilitator helps to form small groups of three to five participants.
- Each small group chooses a topic or issue to explore. Within that group, each participant chooses a different text to read or a different aspect of the topic to research and present.
- The facilitator poses the following questions for brainstorming by the whole group:
  - "As a learner who is not going to read each book or research every aspect of the topic, what information do I want to get from the presenter?"
  - "In what ways would I like that information to be presented—what works best for me as a learner?"
  Ideas emerging from these "learning criteria" brainstorming sessions can be posted on charts, input on a computer and handed out, or e-mailed to each participant as a reminder of "what the learner wants and needs" as participants plan and create their presentations.
- The facilitator ensures that each participant is aware of the parameters of the activity: the length of time allotted for individual presentations and any follow-up questions, the maximum number of pages of any prepared handouts, use of media technology during the presentation, and any photocopying regulations in place.
- At the session in which group members present information individually, the facilitator begins by reviewing the learning criteria developed by the group as a whole and suggests that, after each presentation and follow-up discussion, teachers can also talk about the teaching and learning that was demonstrated. Participants give each other feedback using simple phrases such as:
  - "As a learner, _____ worked for me because _____."
  - "As a learner, I would have liked _____."

Into the Classroom

Besides critiquing the content of the presentation, students can think about and give feedback on presentation criteria that have been developed in advance. The teacher can engage the students in discussing answers to the question: "What makes a good presentation?" Students can draw upon their experiences both as members of an audience to whom a presentation is being given and as presenters themselves. The teacher might also role-play examples of more effective and less effective presentations. Students can also think about how to phrase feedback comments so that the comments are helpful and constructive. They can develop starters that will guide them in offering constructive feedback to presenters, for example: "I really liked it when you…," or "Next time you could…. "

8. Represent Your Reading

This activity encourages each participant to use communication systems other than prose to respond to the text they have read. Participants can progress beyond literal understandings to create new meanings and connections with the text in response modes such as sculpture, dance, music, multimedia formats, and so on.

- Participants are each given a copy of a selection to read. The facilitator leads a discussion about multiple ways to represent meaning and makes a list of possibilities. These possibilities should include familiar classroom activities such as poetry writing, drawing, sculpture, dioramas, singing, and role-playing, as well as less common activities such as baking, knitting, photography, and the use of multimedia materials such as podcasts, electronic slideshows, and websites.
- Participants can work alone or in pairs to create a representation of the text to share at a subsequent session.
- At the next session, each participant (or pair) can share their representation and talk about how it connects to the text they have just read.

This activity can be as simple or as complex as the group wishes. In some cases, the response can be left completely up to the participants, according to their energy level, time, and creativity. At other times, the group can decide to limit the communication formats. For example, suppose a group of teachers is exploring how to support struggling readers in secondary classrooms. Each teacher is asked to read an article and to take a series of photographs of scenes within the school to create a collage that represents a topic discussed in the assigned text. Similarly, each teacher could be asked to bring in an artifact that represented, for them, an important aspect of the text.

Besides creating new meanings and connections and opening up new conversations, this activity can encourage creativity, instill new appreciation for one another's talents, and simply be FUN!!! Laughter cements group cohesion. Can you imagine knitting a response to improving geometry lessons, or singing a rap song about developing a new behavior policy?

Into the Classroom

Possibilities for classroom implementation of this activity with students are limitless because most teachers understand the critical importance of developing activities that appeal to multiple intelligences, for example:
- draw what you feel when you hear this music
- perform a dance to show what it is to be afraid of something
- create blog entries as you read this novel
- demonstrate how this chemical reaction is used in the food industry or in meal preparations

---

Looking Ahead...

Besides the wide range of excellent professional learning materials that can extend and support a teacher's work in the classroom, a myriad of external documents directly impact each teacher's day-to-day planning and teaching. The next chapter discusses how teachers can collaborate to analyze and interpret various external documents that not only guide teaching and learning but also mandate the parameters within which teaching and learning take place.

CHAPTER **3**

Making Sense of External Documents

The work of today's educators is increasingly influenced by expectations external to both the classroom and the school. These expectations take the form of policy documents, resource documents, and curriculum documents published by local school districts, ministries or departments of education, and national associations. Each document establishes parameters within which teachers are expected to function. Familiarity with these parameters is usually an important component of a teacher's work. Teachers benefit from spending time on a regular basis with their colleagues to examine such documents in detail and to explore the effects of the documents on their daily teaching activities.

Curriculum documents appear under many different names, but in most jurisdictions they are referred to as frameworks, guidelines, or learning expectations. These documents are generally subject-specific and they include a detailed list of student learning outcomes, often accompanied by examples, sample questions, and sample issues. They may also include classroom-level learning targets and a philosophy of, rationale for, and/or description of the discipline. The Manitoba Education, Citizenship and Youth website offers the following definition of a curriculum framework:

> A curriculum framework is a subject-specific document which identifies student learning outcomes for what students are expected to know and be able to do as they relate to the knowledge and skills of a particular subject area…. Curriculum frameworks provide the basis for teaching, learning, and assessing in a particular subject area or course. (www.edu.gov.mb.ca/ks4/cur/types.html)

The Manitoba Department of Education also states that standards of achievement or expected levels of student performance in certain subjects such as literacy and mathematics are often included for specific grade levels in order to provide "checkpoints" by means of which the system can monitor overall student progress.

Policy documents set government standards in many broad areas, while **resource documents** (also known as "foundation for implementation documents") support the implementation of those standards. Throughout this chapter, the term "outcomes/standards framework" refers to those curriculum documents that identify the articulated student learning outcomes (sometimes known as learning expectations). These documents usually include relevant classroom-level achievement/learning targets that make up each outcome.

Interpreting a New Policy Document

Several of the activities outlined in Chapter 2 can prove helpful to teachers in their efforts to interpret external policy documents. Policies can cover a wide spectrum of topics affecting the work of teachers and students, topics ranging from teacher supervision to the role of volunteers in schools, from student attendance to equity issues, from acceptable use of technology to student assessment, and so on.

Generally, when a new policy document is released, it has been developed over a relatively long period of time and it has involved discussion throughout the educational system at many committee levels. Once the policy has passed into legislation and has been publicly distributed, all or most teachers are expected to become familiar with the content of the policy and the implications for teaching and learning.

In the following activity, a facilitator uses a version of "inkshedding" to introduce a new policy to a group of educators. This activity could also help familiarize participants with a new resource document.

We meet many dedicated, thoughtful teachers in our graduate courses who tell us that they simply don't have time to do justice to the many policy documents, curriculum guides, and other resources that they receive. It's not that the teachers are negligent or don't care; on the contrary, many express concerns that they are not keeping up. Reading and discussing these resources in the collaborative context of a professional learning community is a workable solution to the time crunch.

- Before the session, the facilitator reviews the policy document and chooses several relevant passages containing key points from the new policy, prints each passage on a separate sheet of chart paper, and posts all the passages for viewing. Participants, alone or in pairs, circulate from chart to chart. They read the passages and respond in writing to express how they think each key point contained in the passages could or should affect their own work—in the classroom, in the learning center, in planning sessions, in communication with parents/guardians, and so on. Participants can also add concerns, questions, or "yes, but…" comments to the charts.
- When everyone has had a chance to respond to the passages in the inkshedding activity, the comments on the charts are shared and discussed item by item. Having been introduced to several key points in a new document in this way, participants then receive their own copies of the policy so they can read the entire text.

In some cases, a group may use this activity to review a curriculum document already in place as a way to highlight specific aspects that appear to be problematic within the school. The facilitator can have participants read and respond individually (and perhaps anonymously) to key points or sections from the document that, in practice, seem to be either unfamiliar to staff or that staff are interpreting in contradictory ways within the school. When listed and shared with the whole group, individual comments can highlight some of the areas that need close attention or further discussion in order to attain consensus among staff in terms of classroom implementation.

Alternatively, participants can use a jigsaw activity (as described in Chapter 2) to help them interpret a new policy, curriculum, or resource document. The document is divided into the same number of sections as there are members in the group. Each member is responsible for reading and reporting on a different section of the document. A chart such as the one on page 39 is reproduced as a blackline master at the back of this book to help teachers structure their note-taking and presentation of ideas. The chart can help facilitate subsequent whole-group discussion as well.

SCENARIO

In the following example, a group of lower elementary teachers have decided to review the NCTE Standards for English Language Arts as one step in their plans to develop a more cohesive language arts program and to help several new teachers on staff gain a better understanding of instructional areas that the school is attempting to improve. Teachers are paired up (a more experienced teacher with a less experienced teacher) and each pair is asked to read, discuss, and report on a different NCTE standard. Pairs fill in the chart below as they work together. (As mentioned previously, a blank version of this chart is included as a blackline master at the back of this book.)

At the end of the session (or at a following session), each pair of teachers has an opportunity to share their responses. Because each pair has dissected a separate standard, they paraphrase the standard in their own words; speculate on what that standard means in terms of interactions within their own classroom, grade level, or school; and list possible strategies or activities that might address the standard. Finally, in the third column of the chart, they list questions and concerns regarding the standard and the new activities that they have suggested.

Study this example of how one pair of teachers might fill in their chart to use in a follow-up discussion with the whole group. Given that there are 12 NCTE Standards for English language arts, the group will end up with a large pool of suggestions and activities to explore at the end of the presentations.

Interpreting Outcomes/Standards

What the Outcome/Standard Says	What the Outcome/Standard Means for "Me/Us" in Terms of the Classroom, Grade Level, and School	Questions/Concerns
Standard 4 is about communication: helping students to develop a sense of audience for their writing, speaking, and presenting. It is also about using appropriate language in different settings for different reasons.	*We need to include more opportunities for students to write for a variety of real audiences, for example:* • *start a writing buddies program between the upper and lower grades in which partners write to and for each other (stories, invitations, blogs, opinion pieces, and so on)* • *for one term this year, try student-led conferences in which students will communicate their own progress to family members or to each other* • *have students create their own newsletters to distribute to their families, describing their favorite subjects, their learning goals, school events, and so on* • *have students write thank-you notes to all guests who have visited the school* • *establish e-mail pals with classes in another school or perhaps in another country* • *other suggestions???*	*For writing opportunities in which students would be communicating to audiences outside the classroom, we would need to discuss how to ensure appropriate use of language conventions such as spelling, grammar, and punctuation.* *What preparation and/or permissions would be necessary to initiate student-led conferences? Check with the principal. Will our parent/guardian community support this kind of assessment at this time?*

Deconstructing Learning Outcomes

Some of the most useful but most often misunderstood documents that guide teachers' work are the outcomes/standards frameworks developed by departments or ministries of education for all subject areas. While these documents provide teachers with an outline of what students are expected to learn in various curriculum areas, they are usually written as general statements pertaining to the learning of all students in all classrooms. Therefore, teachers often perceive these documents as vague and impractical. Teachers need time and collegial support to translate these outcomes into classroom-level student learning or achievement targets that can help teachers clearly understand the underpinnings of each outcome and then articulate clear, detailed, and consistent learning targets for their students.

When this translation process occurs within a school district, a school, or a professional learning community or study group, all those involved develop a sharper understanding of what student achievement of each outcome in various subjects and at various grade levels would look like.

Students can hit any target that holds still for them.
Stiggins, et al., 2004, p. 57

How the Process Works

The process described on the following pages, often referred to as "Deconstructing Outcomes," is based on an activity that appears in work by Richard Stiggins (2008); it also incorporates some aspects of "backwards design" as described in *Understanding by Design* (Wiggins and McTighe, 2005). One of the basic foundations of assessment *for* learning is that the learning targets must be clear for both teachers and students if students are to achieve those targets. In this activity, participants analyze an outcome, identifying and articulating all the achievement/learning targets that students must meet in order to address that outcome.

In many jurisdictions, the outcomes/standards frameworks spell out both the outcomes and the classroom-level learning targets for each outcome. However, even when the outcomes and the learning targets are explicit in the document, it is extremely useful for teachers to work in pairs or small groups to walk through the steps of deconstructing the outcomes for themselves, thereby gaining firsthand knowledge of the scope of the outcomes as well as the nature of the specific learning targets that underpin each outcome.

In situations in which the learning targets for an outcome are explicit and teachers do not wish to deconstruct the outcomes for themselves, teachers can gain a deeper understanding of each outcome by translating the associated learning targets into student-friendly language. Alternatively, they can list all the behaviors and actions that indicate that a student has met a target or outcome, or they can collaborate in devising multiple ways to assess the learning targets associated with each outcome.

Participation in any of these activities will assist teachers in planning the content and/or skills that need to be reviewed, taught, or explored with students. These activities will also help teachers pinpoint more accurately specific areas where a student who is struggling may need additional support. Also, when teachers are completely familiar with the achievement/learning targets necessary to address an outcome, they can create better ways to make those targets clear for their students. And, finally, a clear understanding of the teaching and learning that are implicit in each outcome can improve communication between teachers and students' parents or guardians.

Categorizing Achievement/Learning Targets

Before beginning this activity, teachers must be aware of the many different categories of achievement/learning targets. The categorization of achievement/learning targets and the language used to describe these targets differ from district to district. However, in general, all targets include what students *must know, be able to do,* and *value.* Some outcomes require that students acquire only specific knowledge, while others require more complex learning such as applying the knowledge in specific ways, acquisition of a new skill, or creation of a product.

Stiggins divides learning targets into the following five categories:

1. **Knowledge** (what facts and procedures students need to know)
2. **Reasoning** (what reasoning skills such as classifying, analyzing, comparing, and so on that students must be able to apply)
3. **Skills** (what observable actions students must be able to demonstrate)
4. **Products** (what tangible products students must be able to create)
5. **Dispositions** (what values or attitudes students should be able to express)

As part of this activity, participants can use the blackline master "Deconstructing Outcomes into Classroom-level Achievement/Learning Targets" at the back of this book as is, or modify it to reflect the categorization of reasoning or higher-order thinking skills that is used within their own educational jurisdiction.

In choosing outcomes to deconstruct, teachers may wish to examine outcomes related to their upcoming lesson planning or perhaps outcomes whose wording they find vague or ambiguous compared to others in the outcomes/standards document.

Part 1: Deconstructing Outcomes into Classroom-Level Achievement/Learning Targets

- Teachers work in pairs or small groups to choose an outcome for their grade level or subject area. Using a form such as the one provided on page 104, participants write the outcome at the top of the form and begin by reading it carefully and discussing what knowledge students must have in order to meet that outcome. One participant jots notes in the appropriate "Knowledge" section of the form. *(In Example A, a Grade 5 teacher has determined four things she believes her students will need to know in order to address the outcome successfully.)*
- Participants then move on to the next section and discuss the reasoning skills that students might need to apply in order to meet the outcome. In other words, what will students be required to do with the knowledge outlined in the first section? Many lists of reasoning skills are available in professional books or online, but teachers are encouraged to begin with the outlines provided within district, provincial, or state documents before turning to outside sources. *(In Example A, the teacher has listed*

For a more in-depth description of each of these categories of achievement/learning targets, see *An Introduction to Student-Involved Assessment for Learning* (Stiggins, 2008, pp. 51–67).

Reasoning skills are also known as "higher-order thinking skills," as discussed in the work of Benjamin Bloom (1956).

Note: A skill is observable. To assess a student's ability to accomplish a skill, the teacher/assessor must be able to see the skill in action, whereas a product can be assessed without the student/creator being present. In Example A, the teacher must be able to observe the students as they demonstrate the skill of creating a poem: the poems themselves become the product.

three types of reasoning skills—analysis, interpretation, and comparison—as ways in which students are expected to apply their knowledge.)

- Next, participants discuss what observable skills (if any) students would require to meet the outcome. Here it is important that the skills reflect the outcomes as they are written and NOT the assessment strategy that a teacher may plan to use. For example, for an outcome such as *"students will be expected to demonstrate an understanding of the rights and responsibilities of citizens in a democracy,"* students are expected to attain *knowledge* (what a democracy is, a citizen's rights and responsibilities within a democracy, usually specific to their own country) and demonstrate *reasoning ability* (by analyzing how rights and responsibilities manifest themselves in a citizen's life, and comparing this manifestation with rights and responsibilities in other countries, both democratic and non-democratic). However, no observable skills are required by the outcome. Students may demonstrate their understanding in many forms, for example, in an essay, a speech, a collage, a dance, and so on. As written, the outcome does not specify a required way by which a student must demonstrate achievement of the outcome. *(In contrast, in Example A, part of the outcome indicates that students must create their own poems, thus demonstrating a specific observable skill.)*

- Participants now discuss what products (if any) the students must create in order to achieve the outcome. Again, considering the outcome cited in the previous section, there is no product required by the outcome, but there may be a product required by the teacher's choice of assessment strategy.

- Participants discuss what dispositions (if any) a student would require in order to meet the outcome. *(In Example A, the outcome does not indicate that students must have a specific attitude toward or appreciation for poetry. A student might well be able to demonstrate a mastery of all aspects of this outcome yet still not enjoy or appreciate reading or writing poetry.)*

Part 2: Working with the Learning Targets as Part of the Assessment Process

- After the participants have had a chance to deconstruct an outcome into a list of the relevant knowledge, reasoning, skill, product, and disposition achievement/learning targets, they then translate these targets into "I can…" statements using the language of their students. These "I can…" statements are what the students would be able to say as they accomplish the various achievement/learning targets required by the outcome. Teachers can distribute a list of these statements to students at the beginning of a lesson or a unit to serve as a guide to student progress throughout the lesson or unit. Teachers can post these statements for their students' reference as clear indicators of how well they are doing and what else they need to do in order to meet the outcome. *(In Example A, the teacher posted the "I can…" statements when she introduced the unit, telling the students that by the end of the unit they should be able to make each statement for themselves. As an introductory activity, she had students respond to each statement, commenting on which ones they felt they could already make and which ones they thought they had to learn. This piece of initial writing was filed and referred to at the end of the unit when students were once again asked to respond to each of the statements.)*

- After deconstructing the outcome into classroom-level achievement targets and then rewriting the targets in student-friendly "I can…" statements, participants must think about what student behaviors and actions (i.e., evidence of learning) would indicate that a student has met an outcome or an achievement/learning target. In other words, what should the teacher "look for" as evidence of learning? This step requires that teachers go back to the achievement/learning targets and answer the questions, "How will I know if my students know …?" and/or "What will I observe students being able to do…?" *(In Example A, the teacher lists eight behaviors/actions she believes will tell her that her students have met that outcome. This evidence of learning then becomes the basis of the assessment opportunities she will provide for her students.)*

- Finally, using the list of achievement/learning targets (in both teacher-friendly and student-friendly language) as well as the list of behaviors/actions that the teacher would expect to observe, the participants can design appropriate assessment activities that will allow students to show their learning in a variety of ways. *(In Example A, the teacher creates performance and product-based activities, as well as opportunities to practice both peer and self-evaluation. Depending upon the success of the unit and the extent of student involvement, the poetry readings, either live or taped, could be presented to a variety of audiences.)*

- Pairs or small groups of teachers can share their results in deconstructing different outcomes with other pairs or groups, explaining the process they followed and the connections they made to both teaching and assessment.

SCENARIOS

Following are two real-life examples in which teachers worked through the process of deconstructing outcomes. Note that while teachers were given a copy of the same form to complete (see the blackline master on page 104), each teacher chose to modify the form and to record information in a way that was most useful to that individual. It is also important to note that throughout the process of deconstructing the outcomes into achievement/learning targets, the teachers were encouraged to use their own language rather than the language of the documents.

Example A

In the first example shown on page 45, a Grade 5 teacher has deconstructed two of the Atlantic Provinces English language arts outcomes at her grade level into achievement/ learning targets using teacher-friendly language for herself as well as student-friendly language that she can share with her students. She has chosen to deconstruct the outcomes within the context of a unit on poetry that she plans to teach.

Example B

In the second example, a senior high school mathematics teacher has recorded the deconstruction process quite differently yet effectively for herself (see the chart on page 46). She chose what appeared to be a simple outcome and—while she did not categorize the various achievement/learning targets—she did make a comprehensive list of what the students would need to know as well as what they would need to do in order to meet that outcome.

When she encountered a student who was having difficulty during class, she consulted this list to help her determine exactly where the student's lack of understanding lay. The students themselves found the list of "I will…" statements extremely useful for assessing their own progress. Together, the teacher and the students brainstormed ways in which they could demonstrate their achievement of each statement, thereby involving the students in the assessment process from beginning to end.

Participants can stop at this point to review procedures, share observations, and reflect on the deconstruction process. The next logical step is to use the information to develop instructional activities and to ensure that differentiated instruction and assessment *for* learning are built into every lesson.

While the process of deconstructing outcomes can seem time-consuming and daunting given the sheer number of outcomes, teachers who work through the process several times together find that they begin to think about incorporating outcomes differently in their lesson or unit planning. Groups of teachers working together benefit from the opportunity to share their expectations, their expertise, and their ideas through discussions. The deconstruction process can lead to closer collaboration among teachers and, ultimately, greater consistency for students. Deconstructing outcomes is also a valuable activity for teachers to do as part of developing any school-based common assessments. The process allows a group of teachers to articulate the exact achievement/learning targets that underpin each outcome and to clarify their understandings about what to focus on in each area of learning before deciding what to assess.

Decontextualizing Learning Outcomes

Another way to gain a deeper understanding of outcomes/standards is to have teachers decontextualize outcomes across the curriculum to see patterns of learning that cut across disciplines. Decontextualization allows a school or group of educators to identify the connections between outcomes and to recognize that similar classroom-level achievement targets apply across the curriculum.

In her book *Formative Assessment in Action* (2005), Shirley Clarke provides an activity to clarify learning targets. By separating out learning targets from their context, teachers (and students) begin to grasp how particular learning targets can be applied across the curriculum. Teachers can clearly examine all the targets in various subject areas/disciplines at a particular grade level, by removing the context and pinpointing just the learning targets, for example:

- Be able to investigate a topic using a variety of resources (in science, in health, in math, and other subject areas)
- Be able to show several sides of an issue (a political decision in social studies, character/action analysis in English language arts, the value of new scientific breakthroughs, and so on)
- Be able to communicate (or present) information using a variety of formats for different audiences and purposes (debates in social studies, displays in art, maps in geography, and so on)

Continued on page 48

Deconstructing Outcomes into Classroom-Level Achievement/Learning Targets

Outcomes	Outcome(s) Translated into Classroom-Level Learning Targets	Outcomes Translated into Student-Friendly Language (Statements my students will be able to make at the end of the unit)
From the Atlantic Provinces English Language Arts Grades 4–6 Curriculum Document (1997) *Please note: These outcomes will be applied in the context of a poetry unit.* *1. Students will be able to support their opinions about texts and features of texts.* *2. Students will make deliberate language choices appropriate to purpose, audience, and form, to enhance meaning and achieve interesting effects in imaginative writing and other forms of representing.*	**Knowledge/Understanding** *Students will:* • know what a poem is • know what an opinion is • know a variety of techniques that are often used in poetry • identify characteristics of various forms of poetry (free verse, haiku, shape poem, limerick) **Reasoning** *Students will:* • analyze their own reactions to poems • interpret poems • analyze and compare the effects of various techniques used in the poems read in class **Skills** *Students will be able to:* • find examples of various poetry techniques in the work of others • support their own interpretation of poems with specific references to the text • create several poems using different styles, various poetry techniques, and interesting language **Product(s)** *Students will write different forms of poems demonstrating:* • techniques such as alliteration, onomatopoeia, rhythm, and rhyme • text features specific to poetry (e.g., shape poems, stanzas) • descriptive techniques such as comparison and sensory language	• *I know what a poem is.* • *I know what an opinion is.* • *I know some techniques that poets use.* • *I can name and identify different kinds of poems.* • *I can discuss how a poem makes me feel or what it means to me, and give examples from the poem to back up my opinion.* • *I can talk about how the techniques poets use help me understand the poems or make them interesting to read.* • *I can write different kinds of poems.* • *My poems use some of the same techniques found in the poems we read in class.*

Evidence of Meeting the Outcome(s)/Targets

I will know that students have met the outcome(s)/targets if they:

• can talk about "what makes a poem a poem"
• can tell when a statement is an opinion
• can identify different techniques found in poems
• can discuss the effects of these techniques
• can discuss their interpretation of a poem
• can share their response to a poem
• can provide examples from poems to support their opinions
• can write at least two different forms of poetry, using techniques and features that have been identified as specific to each form

Opportunities for Assessment

Students will be able to demonstrate their understanding through:

• Teacher checklists for observation of class and small group discussion
• Conferences with individual students
• Response journal entries
• Poetry readings
• Student writing folders
• Portfolios
• Class-generated rubrics for peer, self, and teacher assessment of poetry writing assignments

Deconstructing Outcomes into Classroom-Level Achievement/Learning Targets

Outcomes	Outcome(s) Translated into Classroom-Level Learning Targets	Outcome(s) Translated into Student-Friendly Language (Statements my students will be able to make at the end of the unit)
From Atlantic Canada Mathematics Curriculum for Mathematics 10 *Specific Curriculum Outcome (SCO):* By the end of Mathematics 10, students will be expected to "apply the Pythagorean theorem" (D 14)	Students will... 1. know that a right-angled triangle's largest angle is 90° 2. know that a right angle is symbolized as shown below: 3. know that the side of a triangle opposite the 90° angle is called the hypotenuse 4. know how to use letters to label the angles in a triangle and its corresponding sides 5. know that the Pythagorean theorem can only be applied to right-angled triangles 6. know how to square numbers (either mentally or using their calculator) 7. know that the Pythagorean theorem states that "the square of the hypotenuse is equal to the sum of the squares of the two shorter sides" 8. know how to write the formula for the Pythagorean theorem for the triangle under investigation 9. know that the Pythagorean theorem can be used to determine the missing value of the length of one side of a right-angled triangle, if the lengths of the other two sides are known 10. know how to substitute the known values into the formula for the Pythagorean theorem 11. know how to isolate the unknown variable by rearranging the formula 12. know that the square root of a number is a number which when squared will give you the number that you are taking the square root of 13. know how to find the square root of a number (either mentally or using their calculator)	I will... 1. know that a right-angled triangle's biggest angle is 90° 2. know that a 90° angle is represented by the following symbol: 3. know that the side of a triangle directly across from the 90° angle is called the hypotenuse 4. know that capital letters are used to label the angles of a triangle 5. know that the side directly across from an angle is labeled with the same small letter 6. know that the Pythagorean theorem can only be used for a triangle with a 90° angle 7. know that to "square" a number means to multiply it by itself 8. be able to square numbers (either in my head or with the help of a calculator) 9. know that the Pythagorean theorem in words is "if you square the length of the hypotenuse, it is equal to the squares of the lengths of the two shorter sides added together" 10. know how to write the formula for the Pythagorean theorem using the letters that are given in the question (i.e., be able to write the formula for $\triangle ABC$, $\triangle XYZ$, etc.) 11. know that the Pythagorean theorem can be used to find the missing side of any right-angled triangle as long as the other two sides are known 12. know how to replace the known values into the formula for the Pythagorean theorem 13. know how to rearrange the formula to "get the variable by itself" 14. know that when you find the square root of a number, you are looking for a number that, when multiplied by itself, gives you the number you are taking the square root of 15. know how to find the square root of a number (either in your head or with the help of a calculator)

Evidence of Meeting the Outcome(s)/Targets	Opportunities for Assessment
I will know that students have met the achievement/learning targets when…	Students will be able to demonstrate their understanding through…
1. they can write an appropriate formula for any right-angled triangle	1. completion of in-class practice sheets
2. they can substitute in the known values correctly	2. completion of take-home practice sheets
3. they can rearrange the formula correctly in order to isolate the variable	3. whole-class discussions (e.g., being able to answer questions that the teacher asks during whole-class instruction)
4. they can correctly determine the length of a missing side in any right-angled triangle	4. one-on-one discussions (e.g., being able to answer questions during individual conversations)
	5. individual assignments
	6. group work (e.g., practice sheets, group assignments, etc.)
	7. tests/quizzes
	8. applying the Pythagorean theorem in word problems

- Be able to classify objects into categories (e.g., geometric figures in mathematics, plants in science, land forms in geography)
- Be able to follow directions (e.g., conducting an investigation in science, finding a location in orienteering in physical education, constructing a net in mathematics, making a casserole in life studies)
- Be able to write/create directions (e.g., recipes, laboratory investigations, geographical locations)
- Be able to use specific tools or apparatus in a safe manner (e.g., in the science laboratory, technology lab, woodworking class, or art class)
- Be able to use information to solve a problem (e.g., in mathematics, health, or science)

As one example of learning outcomes decontextualization, Church, Baskwill, and Swain (2007) describe the development of a cross-curricular unit at the junior high level, during which each subject-area teacher examined the use of literacy strategies within several disciplines. "The teachers' goal was to help students understand that learning to use such strategies [brainstorming, graphic organizers, concept webs, text features] in one area would help them in other areas." (p. 91). Each teacher reviewed the outcomes framework for their subject and selected literacy-related outcomes. The following chart shows how each of the subjects featured similar literacy-related outcomes that the teachers could translate into cross-curricular instructional approaches.

Applying Insights

Professional learning communities provide an effective forum in which teachers can, in collaboration with their colleagues, cope effectively and practically with the plethora of documents relating to policy and curriculum. Analyzing and interpreting documents in a way that reflects the kind of learning—collegial, collaborative, and relevant—that they strive to create for their own students is an essential and productive undertaking.

Chapter 4 offers many suggestions for applying the insights developed in the course of analyzing, deconstructing, and decontextualizing policy, curriculum, and resource documents. When examining student work, teachers can draw upon their ever-expanding knowledge of classroom-level achievement/learning targets to assess their students' growth as learners.

Subject	Related Literacy Goals Students will be expected to…	Teacher Instruction
Science	1. select and integrate information from various print and electronic sources 2. identify new questions and problems that arise from what is learned 3. communicate questions, ideas, intentions, plans, and results using point-form notes, sentences, data tables, graphs, drawings, oral language, and other means	• promoted the use of numerous sources of information on a topic • provided a wide variety of written science materials, including popular science magazines, government and scientific reports, newspaper articles, website addresses • demonstrated strategies for reading difficult scientific texts • shared samples of scientists' journals • demonstrated the use of graphic organizers and note-taking matrices • helped students prepare questions to interview scientists and other experts
Social Studies	1. ask complex geographic questions 2. acquire, organize, and analyze geographic information and answer geographic questions 3. analyze selected issues to illustrate the interdependence among people, technology, and the environment	• demonstrated strategies for reading complex texts • demonstrated the use of graphic organizers and note-taking matrices • encouraged students to seek primary sources of information • encouraged students to look at topics from various perspectives—political, big business, small business, uninformed citizenry, financial, etc.
Mathematics	1. solve problems involving the collection, display, and analysis of data 2. interpret information from their graphs	• provided students with opportunities to learn and use the language of data and statistics • helped students to learn to read problems carefully
English Language Arts	1. communicate information and ideas effectively and clearly, and respond personally and critically 2. interact with sensitivity and respect, considering the audience and purpose 3. interpret, select, and combine information using a variety of strategies, resources, and technologies 4. respond critically to a range of texts, applying their understanding of language, form, and genre 5. use a range of strategies to develop effective writing and other ways of representing, and to enhance their clarity, precision, and effectiveness	• provided students with samples of scientific papers to examine and develop related criteria • posted student-generated criteria for the various formats and encouraged them to use the guidelines to self-assess throughout the process • helped students to brainstorm questions about their topic before researching • facilitated students' use of visual supports (diagrams, graphs, charts, labeled drawings, etc.) and organizational supports (indexes, tables of contents, glossaries, text boxes, titles, etc.) to read technical texts • worked with groups of students to develop interviewing techniques and ways to write up the information • set up and monitored peer editing groups • met with project groups regularly, going over their proposals, their progress, and any group problems • met with individuals to help them set goals and timelines for themselves, particularly those students with organizational difficulties • encouraged students to role play situations in which each group member would take a different perspective on their issue • taught lessons on how to cite reference materials correctly

CHAPTER **4**

Examining Student Work

In the run of a day, teachers spend a great deal of time examining and responding to students' work. They gather information and draw conclusions about what the learner already knows and can do, the kind of feedback students need, and what instruction students should receive. Teachers also engage in critical reflection regarding their own practices, asking themselves questions such as:

- How appropriate was this task for this learner?
- Could I have provided a different kind of support to help the learner be more successful?
- How might I change my instruction based on my observations of this student's work?

Classroom assessment for learning is an integral part of the teaching/learning process. When teachers meet in small professional learning groups to examine student work, they enjoy the advantage of being able to slow the process down, to focus on a small sample of work, and to benefit from their collective observations and reflections. Once away from their busy classrooms, they can think deeply about what students' work has to teach them about student learning and then consider the implications for their classroom practices. As noted in the conclusion to Chapter 3, developing a deeper understanding of standards/outcomes will greatly enrich the analysis of student work samples. Teachers can consider student work samples relative to the achievement targets, determining how well students are doing and where they might need additional support.

Protocols for Examining Student Work

The development and refinement of protocols for examining student work as part of school change efforts has been the focus of a study group comprising both individuals and organizations that was established in the late 1990s. The Looking at Student Work Association (www.lasw.org) frames its inquiries according to a number of key principles, summarized as follows:

1. Student work is like that of adults: it is serious, intentional, meant for an audience, and it appears in multiple genres and forms.
2. The examination of student work is an inquiry process in which the focus is to learn; student work provides key data that drive school change.
3. The collaborative examination of student work helps teachers to develop greater consistency in their assessment and makes their work public.

4. The process of examining student work needs to be in-depth, over time, collaborative, and critically reflective.
5. When teachers examine student work together, there needs to be coherence among the purpose for looking, the type of work being examined, and the process used for examining student work (in other words, the protocol).
6. Conversations about student work need to take place in the context of a clear understanding of outcomes/standards (personal, local, community, and national).
7. Looking at student work connects student learning and the work of the school (in terms of curriculum, instruction, policies, and other important aspects).

One of the challenges in examining student work is to resist moving to evaluative statements too quickly. Keeping the conversation as open and inquiring as possible will lead to the discovery of unexpected insights into students' learning and teachers' practices.

How a professional learning community group actually carries out their examination of student work will vary depending upon their purposes and the nature of the work. There are, however, a number of consistent procedures that group members can follow:

- An individual teacher or group of teachers brings forward a small selection of student work to be examined in a meeting.
- Someone other than the presenter(s) facilitates the meeting.
- The facilitator leads the group through an agreed-upon protocol for examining the work; the protocol outlines roles, procedures, guiding questions, and time frames.
- Norms for inquiry focus on the evidence that is inherent in the work, discovery of patterns, respectful listening, rigorous questioning, consideration of different perspectives, exploration of assumptions underlying these perspectives, and self- and group reflection.
- The group conducts a debriefing session on the entire process.

Choosing Student Work Samples

When teachers offer examples of student work for collaborative examination, they are in effect opening a window into their own teaching practices. How students perform reflects on teachers' perceptions of their own performance and exposes them to the evaluative judgments of others. Therefore, it is extremely important to move slowly into conversations about student work and to follow protocols that emphasize collective learning from the students' work rather than evaluation of the teacher. Furthermore, it may be helpful in the initial stages to examine samples that are not identified with a particular teacher. Practicing with student work from another school or from an online source—for example, a teachers' network, a ministry/department of education website, or a professional association website—can help a professional learning group develop essential levels of trust, discussion skills, and analytical processes before tackling student work generated in their own classrooms.

The type of work chosen can be any product that offers possibilities for discussion and reflection. Student work can take many different forms: writing across a range of genres; mathematical problems; projects; reports; presentations; portfolios; student-designed websites; audiotapes, videotapes, or photographs of presentations or performances; and transcripts of oral reading.

When teachers bring forward samples of student work to be examined and discussed, their choices should raise questions for them and represent something they want to learn more about by seeking the input of others. When participants present student work to the group, they should

1. ensure that student names are removed
2. make enough copies of written samples for everyone and think about how best to present products such as artwork, portfolios, or videos
3. provide supporting documents such as curriculum outcomes/standards, assignment descriptions, or rubrics related to the task
4. present a brief overview of the context within which the sample was created
5. provide a focusing question (see the next page for examples of focusing questions)

The presenter(s) can bring forward one sample or multiple samples, depending upon their needs and purposes. Some possibilities include:

- one student's responses to different assignments
- samples of a student's work over time
- responses of several different individuals or groups (for example, in the form of a collaborative project or presentation) to the same assignment
- responses from one student who was successful with an assignment and one who was not successful
- responses to similar assignments from different classrooms at the same grade level
- responses to a particular type of task across grade levels, for example, descriptive writing from Grades 3 to 6 or Grades 9 to 12

 Web 2.0—Accessing Exemplars of Student Work

Numerous sources of student work exemplars are available online. Many government assessment branches provide easy access to such samples, which can be located through a simple Internet search. Using student exemplars for practice is an excellent way for a group to begin an ongoing process of examining student work. In most cases, the exemplars are clearly connected to the outcomes/standards that they exemplify and the exemplars represent different levels of students' performance relative to those standards. A professional learning community can examine the work of their own students in relationship to these exemplars, further developing their insights into student learning and their understanding of the external expectations.

Talking to Learn

Talking to learn is quite different from talking to get things done, to socialize, or to reach closure. When examining student work, participants need to adopt an inquiring stance, keeping their minds open to one another's perspectives. A discussion related to student work may not always result in agreement. Instead, it

Here are the principles I've learned to emphasize before we begin a formal conversation process: we acknowledge each other as equals; we try to stay curious about each other; we recognize that we need each other's help to become better listeners; we slow down so we have time to think and reflect; we remember that conversation is the natural way humans think together; we expect it to be messy at times.
Wheatley, 2002, p. 29

may lead to further inquiry regarding areas in which there are multiple interpretations of the evidence of learning.

For example, suppose that in a collection of a student's writing over several months the most recent samples show errors in conventions that the student appeared to have used appropriately earlier in the year. Possible interpretations of this discrepancy might include: the student is getting careless; the student needs some reteaching of conventions; the later writing represents beginning drafts for which the student believed conventions did not matter; the student was trying a new genre or focusing on style and therefore did not attend to conventions temporarily.

Rather than reaching a hasty conclusion, a professional learning community needs to consider all of the possibilities, describing what they see in the student's collected writing and exploring the questions that arise during the group discussion. As a result of the discussion, the presenter might return to the classroom to gather more information through observation and interaction with the learner. The discussion might also affect the practices of other participants as they reconsider their interpretations of evidence from student writers in their own classrooms.

Asking Effective Questions to Promote Thoughtful Discussions

Posing questions and discussing alternative responses to those questions is at the heart of collaborative examination of student work. It takes practice to become skilled in engaging in these kinds of conversations. Protocols that include the types of questions that generate rich discussions are extremely helpful. In the early stages of meeting as a group, it may be beneficial to have a trained facilitator lead the group and assist them in learning how to use questioning effectively. Often, district-level staff development departments have consultants with this kind of expertise available. University and community college faculties can also provide assistance in this area.

The Looking at Student Work Association identifies several different kinds of questions that professional learning communities can use flexibly to promote thoughtful discussions. (A list of helpful "Questions to Guide Examination of Student Work" is included as a blackline master at the back of this book.)

- The big issues that are of interest to the group and that group members tend to explore over time often focus around broad **inquiry questions.** Examples include: How can we increase students' reading and writing of nonfiction texts? How can we use collaborative small group learning in high school social studies and science to help students develop critical thinking skills?
- Discussion centred around a sample or samples of student work brought forward for examination is guided by **focusing questions.** An individual presenter may pose a question regarding a sample or samples, or the group may develop a focusing question to use in looking at a number of samples from different classrooms. These questions can relate to
  - the quality of the student work: How well does this sample meet the criteria for the assignment?
  - teaching practices: Based on the students' responses, how appropriate was this assignment for these learners? What could be done to make the assignment more appropriate?

- students' understanding: What evidence is there in students' science journals that they understand scientific observation?
  - students' growth: How can I encourage students to take more risks in their writing?
  - students' intent and motivation: What evidence is there that the student found this task engaging? What was the student trying to achieve?
- Participants use **clarifying questions** to obtain more information from the presenter, for example:
  - How many days were the students given to work on this project?
  - Did the students work independently or in groups?
  - What prior experiences did the students have before beginning this science inquiry?
- More in-depth, **probing questions** foster deeper thinking about the students' work and the issues that arise from the evidence of learning. Participants need to monitor themselves to ensure that they do not already have a preconceived answer in mind; that the questions relate to the focus identified by the presenter; that the questions are inquiring, not blaming; and that the questions invite the presenter to consider different possibilities for what the work reveals and how that might affect their teaching practices in the future. Examples of probing questions include:
  - Why did you structure the assignment this way?
  - What would happen if you changed the group members?
  - Have you experienced anything like this before?
  - What do you think you would have to change to help students take more responsibility for their own learning?
- At the end of the discussion, **reflective questions** shift attention to the overall student work examination process in which participants have engaged:
  - What went well?
  - What did we learn?
  - Are we getting better at asking probing questions?
  - Did the discussion contribute to insights into our inquiry question?
  - How might we improve the process next time?

  Individual participants can also pose reflective questions, for example:
  - What did I learn that was surprising or interesting?
  - What new perspectives did colleagues offer?
  - How will these perspectives help me to grow as a teacher?
  - What additional questions did the discussion raise for me?
  - What new strategies will I try out in my classroom as a result of looking at this student work?

Protocols for Structuring Discussions About Student Work

Research related to examining student work strongly supports the use of protocols. Protocols are similar to lesson plans that provide a framework to guide the discussion. Professional learning communities can draw upon the experiences of other seasoned educators by experimenting with and adapting existing protocols. (The Recommended Resources list at the back of this book includes several sources for such protocols.) Outlined on the following pages are some suggestions for simple protocols that may serve as viable ways for groups to structure discussions about student work.

1. Notice and Describe

Using one or several samples of student work, this protocol helps teachers to look at evidence of learning with open minds and to describe the evidence impartially. The purpose of this protocol is to encourage teachers to learn as much as possible about the student's thinking on the basis of thoughtful and dispassionate examination of products. Before applying this protocol to examination of a student work sample presented by a group member, the group may find it helpful to examine a very short piece of student writing or a drawing to practice using descriptive words and phrases only. *It is important to keep the language descriptive, rather than evaluative.*

- The presenter describes the context in which the work was produced. Less information tends to result in more open description as too much prior knowledge regarding the work and/or the student may influence what participants see and how they interpret what they see.
- The facilitator invites each participant to describe one thing they notice about the work, going around the group several times; another person records the comments on chart paper. Participants may pass if they wish and there is no dialogue about the comments.
- After a number of rounds, the group reviews the recorded comments and discusses what they have learned about the student. At this point, participants may ask clarifying questions, and the presenter may wish to ask a focusing question to take the discussion further.
- Individuals and groups can then consider reflective questions such as:
  - Why do I (we) see the students' work this way?
  - What assumptions underlie my (our) observations?
  - What is important to me (us)?

2. Make a "Can Do" List

Reviewing a sample or samples of student work for the purposes of determining what the student can do puts emphasis on the positive aspects of teaching and learning. This protocol prompts teachers to look for evidence of what the student is doing well and provides information to guide future instruction.

- Distribute a sample of student work with a brief description of the context in which it was produced.
- Ask participants to make a list of everything that the student can do and then compile a group list of these "can do's."
- Repeat this activity with samples from different subjects and from a wide array of students.
- Follow up the "can-do" discussion with consideration of what feedback a teacher might offer the student and what might constitute the next step in learning. What kind of instruction would best support this student's growth as a learner?

The example on page 58 shows how a teacher used a "can-do" format to assess two pages from six-year-old Jillian's journal (shown below). (A blank "Can-Do Writing Assessment Form" is included as a blackline master at the back of this book.)

3. Sort, Categorize, and Describe

Using this protocol, the group examines the responses of all the students in a class to the same assignment. The purpose is to generate discussion about the criteria that group members can devise to determine what constitutes successful performance.

- The presenter collects a class set of responses to an assignment, providing a brief description of the context in which the work was produced. Each (anonymous) sample should be labeled with a letter or a number. If possible, each participant should receive a set of photocopied samples. Alternatively, the participants can work in pairs or small groups, sharing sets of samples.
- Each individual (pair or small group) sorts the samples into three categories: high quality, middle-level quality, and poor quality. They record the number or letter of the samples in each category on chart paper and then make a list of the criteria that they used to categorize the samples.
- Each person (pair or small group) shares the results of their sorting and the criteria that they used with the whole group.
- Discussion focuses on commonalities and differences in establishing sorting decisions and criteria. The purpose of this discussion is to compare perceptions and beliefs about what constitutes success. The group may discover that there is consensus among participants regarding some samples but differences in opinion regarding other samples.

Can-Do Writing Assessment Form

Student's Name: _Jillian_   Age: _6_   Grade: _Primary/Kindergarten_

Date of Sample: _May 12, 2009_   Teacher: _M. Crocker_

Context of the Writing Activity:

Format: _Journal entry_   Audience: _Self and to share with teacher_

In a special journal scribbler, 6-year-old Jillian writes each day about things that happen

to her or interest her. At regular times, she shares the scribbler with her teacher who often

writes back comments about the things that Jillian has written.

Evidence of What the Writer CAN DO:

Writes left to right

Knows about words—leaves spaces between words in her sentences

Knows about sentences—expresses complete, single thoughts

Uses periods to end most sentences

Creates illustrations to match and extend the text

Uses several spelling strategies—sight words (she, had, in, he, a) and letter/sounds (dansin,

lodstr, butifol, mos, bab, bocs)

Demonstrates a sense of storytelling—provides action, clear sequence, relevant details

Uses imagination and her own experiences to create interesting stories (i.e., a tap dancing

lobster—Jillian is taking tap dancing lessons herself)

Capitalizes "I"

Number of running words used: _19 words_   Spelling accuracy (%): _10/19 or 53%_

Evaluator: _M. Crocker_   Date: _June 15, 2009_

- The group might choose one or two of the contentious samples and engage in further discussion about what people perceive in the sample that led them to the decisions that guided their sorting. The goal is not to reach consensus but to examine which characteristics of the sample or which underlying assumptions led to different sorting decisions.
- To take the discussion further, the group might consider the samples in relationship to school, district, or national outcomes/standards to determine how the juxtaposition of these accountability frameworks might influence their decisions regarding student performance. (See Chapter 3 for activities related to analyzing curriculum outcomes/standards.)

4. Look for Patterns Across Grade Levels

A cross-grade level group of teachers can examine a collection of representative samples of students' responses to a similar task from each grade level. For example, teachers at the Grades 3 to 6 level might look at samples of descriptive writing. As another example, high school social studies teachers might look at samples from across high school courses and grades that demonstrate evidence of students' ability to synthesize information from primary and secondary sources.

- Before examining student work, the group should clarify their goals related to the area of student learning that is the focus of discussion. For example:
  - What do we want students to be able to do in terms of descriptive writing?
  - What are the features of effective descriptive writing?
  - What evidence of effective descriptive writing should we see in student work?
- Each teacher collects a range of five or six samples that represent the full spectrum of student responses, from highly successful to least successful.
- The group examines each grade-level set of samples, discussing what students are able to do and where they seem to be struggling.
- Then the group considers the samples as a whole, looking for patterns and evidence of growth across the grades.
- The group reflects on the implications for instruction:
  - What seems to be going well?
  - Where do we need to put more emphasis?
  - How might we address the needs of students who seem to be struggling with this area of learning?
  - How might we challenge students who are doing well to take the next step in learning?
  - How can we create more coherence and consistency in our teaching from grade to grade or from course to course?

5. Take a Slice

A 1996 project conducted by the Bush Educational Leadership Program at the University of Minnesota developed a process that the project leaders called "taking a slice." A slice is a collection of all the work produced by students over a designated time period, for example, over one or two days or over a longer period, if that is manageable. Depending on the purposes established for the discussion, the collection can be distributed over several classes, or it can focus on one grade level or on a particular group of students such as those receiving special education services. The collection should include all written work and responses to assignments, as well as any videotapes, audiotapes, and photographs.

Logistically, it can be challenging to create a slice because teachers must collect the material, remove student names, and copy and organize the material in a usable way. Collecting the material and removing student names are tasks that must be undertaken by a teacher or an administrator. However, a parent volunteer, teacher's aide, or upper-grade student could assist with the time-consuming job of preparing the packages.

- The group must decide on a focusing question for their examination of the slice, for example: "What does this work tell us about our efforts to engage students actively in learning?" "Are we providing a diverse range of opportunities for different types of learners?" "What does this collection reveal about the purposes for student learning?"
- The presenter provides a brief description of the collection, providing information on how and from what type of learner it was collected and during what time frame.
- Participants review the work with the focusing question in mind, making notes. The samples may be divided among several smaller groups so that everything can be reviewed within a reasonable time frame.
- The facilitator leads a discussion about the findings of the participants in relationship to the focusing question and then invites reflection on the implications for instruction.

6. Take on the Student Role

When working with pre-service teachers who are just learning to design lessons, we often challenge them to complete the tasks that they have designed for their students. Frequently they discover problems such as unclear purpose, vague instructions, or complexity beyond the learners' capabilities. Prospective English teachers are much less likely to ask junior high students to write a short story when they have tried to craft an effective one themselves!

Teachers can gain insights into the demands that a task places on students by completing the assignment themselves and examining both the students' responses and their own responses.

- The group chooses an assignment and collects student responses to the assignment from one or more classrooms.
- Before examining the student work, each group member completes the assignment themselves and the group debriefs afterwards with discussion centred on how they experienced the task as learners.
  - Were teachers clear about what was expected?
  - What prior learning was required in order to complete the task?
  - To what extent did the assignment accomplish the intended purpose?
  - To what extent was the assignment engaging?
- The group can then examine the students' responses to the assignment, bearing in mind the perceptions and insights they gained when they put themselves in the role of learners. When making observations about the student products, the teachers can take into consideration how features of the assignment (such as length, format, clarity of instructions, or complexity of language) might have influenced both the students' abilities to handle the task and the quality of their responses.
- The discussion can then advance to how to revise the assignment to make it more supportive of students' growth and the accomplishment of the intended purposes.

Examination of Student Work to Guide Instruction

This chapter has provided several practical suggestions and protocols related to ways in which teachers can use their analysis of student work to guide instruction. After discussing and reflecting on the insights and questions regarding student learning that result from careful examination of work samples, the next step is to consider the implications for teaching.

Students' responses reveal a great deal about the nature of the instruction that they have received and, therefore, can help teachers make thoughtful and informed decisions about ways to improve their teaching practices in the future. Chapter 5 focuses directly on these classroom practices, offering suggestions for how teachers can work together to enhance and expand their repertoire of instructional strategies.

CHAPTER **5**

Rethinking Teaching Practices

As every teacher knows, making changes in teaching practices is difficult and challenging. It is not easy to give up familiar strategies and to adopt different ways of teaching. In a supportive and trusting professional learning community, however, teachers can work through desired changes together, drawing on what they already know and building new knowledge and insights. Activities that focus on a critical analysis of "what's going on here?" help teachers gain insights into the complexities associated with teaching and learning. Over time, professional learning communities can develop a culture of inquiry in which ongoing critical reflection about teaching practices is the norm—an integral part of being a teacher.

In a culture of inquiry, teachers are not looking for "right" answers or for the latest "silver bullet" teaching technique. Instead, they are engaged in identifying, exploring, and solving problems together. They continually monitor how well their instruction is supporting student learning and search for ways to change what they are doing to address areas of need. They become informed about current research and consider its implications for their teaching. They share their practices with colleagues and are open to learning from their colleagues' perspectives. They know how to offer and receive constructive criticism. And, finally, they conduct their professional lives with high levels of trust and professional respect toward others.

Effective Ways to Examine Teaching Practices

The following activities are designed to help professional learning communities to inquire into teaching practices and to explore new possibilities for teaching and learning.

1. Reviewing Demonstration Lessons

Reviewing lessons designed and taught by teachers outside the professional learning community can reduce the feelings of risk that may be associated with reviewing demonstration lessons emerging from teachers' own classrooms. Furthermore, examining the work of others beyond the professional learning community is a means of connecting with a larger educational context: the profession as a whole.

There are many examples of lesson plans and videos of demonstration lessons available from a variety of sources. Professional books and journals often include sample lessons and descriptions of classroom practices. In recent years, publishers have increasingly added video material in either CD or DVD format to professional books, and there are many stand-alone professional development resources that feature video components. A professional learning community might draw upon videos of a number of different demonstration lessons with a similar focus and view each demonstration lesson critically, identifying strengths and weaknesses.

While not a substitute for actual classroom observation, these virtual visits to someone else's teaching environment, followed by collaborative analyses, can help to inform teachers' own lesson designs, expanding creative possibilities and offering alternative ways of thinking about a particular aspect of teaching.

Web 2.0—Accessing Lesson Ideas and Examples

The Internet is a source of many lesson plans and demonstration lessons that can serve as a good focus of analysis. A search will yield literally thousands of sites. Teachers must exercise their professional judgment when choosing lessons to review. (Questions to consider when reviewing lesson plans are provided in the blackline master "What Makes a Good Lesson Plan?" at the back of this book.) The websites of professional organizations, such as those listed on page 22 in Chapter 1, are excellent repositories of reliable, high-quality lessons. These sites often feature links to other relevant resources. For example, the International Reading Association and the National Council of Teachers of English jointly sponsor a site (www.readwritethink.org) that contains peer-reviewed language/literacy lessons and student activities for Grades K to 12, as well as links to other sites offering high-quality lesson plans and activities.

When a professional learning community has chosen to focus on a particular aspect of teaching—for example, problem solving in mathematics, conducting writing conferences, researching questions in social studies or science, or any other area of practice—it is helpful to examine the different ways by means of which teachers plan and carry out instruction. The group might begin by collecting a number of lesson plans and/or accessing videotaped lessons and then discussing the assumptions about teaching and learning reflected in the examples, as well as the strengths and weaknesses of each of the lessons. The group can consider questions such as:

- To what extent does the lesson reflect our beliefs about learning and teaching?
- In what ways does the lesson support students' progression toward the achievement of standards?
- How well would this lesson support the specific learning needs of our students?
- How might we revise the lesson to make it more effective?

2. Critiquing Instructional Materials

The instructional resources that teachers use in their classrooms have a significant impact on what and how they teach. Teaching guides and student materials shape what teachers do and say and how students experience learning. As part of teachers' inquiries into teaching practices, they can gather useful information through a critical examination of these resources. They can determine to what extent the resources support curricular goals and students' achievement of expected outcomes/standards. By conducting such analyses together, teachers can become more informed consumers of instructional resources.

Teachers can structure their conversations about instructional resources by considering the following questions:

- To what extent and how clearly do the resources articulate the purposes and goals of the program? To what extent do the stated goals match my (our) beliefs about teaching and learning? To what extent do the stated goals match the philosophy of the school, district, or province/state?
- What pedagogical orientation is dominant in the resource?
- How flexible is the resource? Can it be adapted to different teaching situations or is it so tightly structured that it can be delivered in only one way?
- How well will this resource support the specific needs of our learners? To what extent does the program appeal to students from diverse cultural, linguistic, and social backgrounds?
- Do the assessment components in the resource support ongoing classroom assessment that helps to inform instruction and guide student learning? Are there specific suggestions for viable ways in which teachers can gather assessment information? Are tools such as rubrics, checklists, and assessment criteria included in the resource? Are there suggestions for student self- and peer assessment?
- Do the materials appear engaging to both teachers and students?
- To what extent will the resource help us address the area of teaching that is our chosen focus?
- What do we see as the resource's overall strengths and weaknesses?

3. Sharing Best Practices

Teachers are typically highly self-critical so they may feel uncomfortable talking about their work in terms of "best practices." Once they move past that initial discomfort, however, the process can become a source of encouragement, positive feedback from peers, and professional affirmation.

Every teacher can identify aspects of their teaching that have been highly effective in helping students to learn and that have contributed to students' attainment of intended outcomes. These "best practices" can become the focus of discussions and analysis in a collaborative learning community. The presenters have an opportunity to share positive aspects of their work, and both presenters and the rest of the group can gain deeper insights into the factors that contribute to successful teaching. Sharing is best done in groups of three or four so that everyone has a chance to present and receive feedback.

- Each presenter writes a brief description of a best practice, including an explanation of why the practice has been successful and what differentiates it from other teaching situations.
- After the presenter shares this description, other group members can ask clarifying questions.
- The group discusses the presenter's interpretations of the practice and adds further insights. The presenter responds to the analysis.
- The group celebrates the success of the presenter.
- Others then take turns sharing their best practices.
- The group explores how they might apply what they have learned when planning future learning experiences, considering questions such as:
  - What factors contribute to the creation of a best practice?
  - How can we replicate those factors in a variety of teaching contexts?

SCENARIO

A professional learning community of Grades 7 and 8 English and social studies teachers at a middle school had been working on how to help their students become more critical readers, writers, and thinkers. They decided that each teacher would share a best practice from their classroom. When it was her turn, Sarah, one of the Grade 8 English teachers, wrote the following description of her best practice:

> I've always done a media unit as part of my curriculum, but I have been finding that many teachers at earlier grades address media, so the students have already experienced many of the sorts of activities that I typically include in my unit. I was also concerned at how stereotypically my young adolescent students view gender roles. Therefore, I decided to reconfigure the curriculum as an inquiry into how gender is constructed through popular media. It required a lot of planning on my part. I formulated a large inquiry question: "How are males and females portrayed in the media?" I then led the class through a set of media awareness activities. I designed and implemented a four-week unit that engaged my students in working in small groups to investigate aspects of the inquiry question. I helped each of the groups to develop their own smaller inquiry question, focused on an aspect that interested them. Over three weeks the students worked in small groups to investigate their questions using a project framework that I provided. The unit culminated with small groups presenting their information in creative ways using multimedia. Despite the growing pains that the students and I experienced—mainly because they needed more support than I had anticipated in working effectively in groups and in directing their own learning—I consider this experience a best practice for the following reasons:
> - Over the four weeks the students became much more skilled at working together productively.
> - Each of the groups developed a question that caused them to read, write, and think critically.
> - There was a higher level of student engagement than I had ever seen with this group of students.
> - I was run off my feet but was energized and excited about teaching this way.
> - The students' final products were the most creative and carefully executed projects I have seen from a group of Grade 8 students.

Sarah shared a few of the final products—a video, a magazine, and a radio play—that demonstrated her students' learning. In the ensuing discussion, the other teachers shared what they observed in the products, asked Sarah to talk more about the specifics of her plan, and shared their own experiences working with students on similar projects. They agreed with Sarah's reasons for considering this unit a best practice and added a few more factors accounting for the success of the unit:

- the teacher engaged in careful pre-planning
- she activated her students' prior knowledge and experience
- she provided scaffolding for the students (the inquiry framework, guidelines for the project, and assessment criteria)
- she adapted the instruction as needed

As a follow-up, the group decided to bring examples of frameworks for inquiry that they had developed in both English and social studies contexts. They also agreed that it would be helpful to learn more about classroom organization and management approaches that work well with student self-directed projects.

4. Creating a Classroom Collage

Advance preparation is required for this activity that involves the creation of a collage representing the classroom of a teacher who is not a member of the professional learning community. Using an example from outside the group prevents this activity from becoming an evaluation of one of the group members. The collage might include photographs showing the classroom configuration, teaching/learning materials, displays on walls and bulletin boards, and students at work. It can also include samples of student work. The collage can be constructed on a bulletin board in the staff meeting room or on several sheets of poster board.

Assuming responsibility for the construction of the collage is one way in which an administrator—principal, vice-principal, or department head—can support the professional learning community tangibly. The school can also enlist the help of a curriculum consultant or lead teacher. It might be possible for a professional learning community in one school to partner with a neighboring school and for each school to prepare a collage for the other group to discuss. This approach has the advantage of involving all the members of the community in task preparation. In situations in which high levels of trust exist among the members of a professional learning community, one of the teachers may volunteer to construct and share a classroom collage with the group.

Whatever the approach, participants should have the opportunity to examine the collage at the beginning of a session and to make notes on their observations. What do they notice about the classroom? How creatively does this teacher use space and resources? What and how are students learning? After everyone has had an opportunity to make individual observations, the group can discuss questions such as:

- What beliefs about teaching and learning are reflected in this classroom? What evidence in the collage supports each interpretation of teachers' beliefs?
- What inferences can be drawn about the nature of student-teacher interactions in this classroom?
- What insights regarding our own classrooms can we derive by examining this collage?

After discussing the collage representing another teacher's classroom, members of the professional learning community may wish to create collages of their own classrooms and bring them forward to the group for discussion. Such collages can become an effective means of communication with parents or guardians during meetings with family members on curriculum nights or in parent-teacher interviews. Classroom collages are a means of extending the learning beyond the collaborative teacher group to involve family members in discussing how the classroom supports their children's learning.

5. Observing in Classrooms

Once trust has been established within a professional learning community, the members can learn a great deal by observing what goes on in each other's classrooms. Logistically, peer observation can pose problems since it is difficult to arrange schedules in such a way that a teacher can spend time in a colleague's classroom and both teachers can have an opportunity for discussion before and after the visit. Clearly, school administrators can play an essential role in addressing these logistical issues.

Principals can schedule specialist teachers' teaching time (for music classes, physical education classes, etc.) and classroom teachers' preparation time to release teachers from teaching responsibilities, thus creating opportunities for peer observation and discussion. Some principals make it a priority to devote some of their own time to take over teachers' classrooms so that visits to a peer's classroom can occur. Within a school in which collaboration is highly valued and well established, teachers may be willing to use their prep time to cover for a colleague who is observing in another classroom, knowing that someone will do the same for them on another occasion.

When logistics make it extremely difficult to arrange visits, teachers with access to video equipment may be able to capture and share some of their classroom dynamics and teaching practices through video-recording, and then discuss the video with a peer. This method may work well if the focus is on a specific aspect of teaching, such as teacher questioning, that is relatively easy to follow with a video camera. Bear in mind that capturing the highly interactive and dynamic context of the classroom as a whole is far more complex, even for professional videographers.

When teachers invite peers into their classrooms to make observations, they expose their work to the scrutiny of another professional. No matter how trusting the relationships among peers, some teachers will undoubtedly experience feelings of insecurity and even a reluctance to participate. Therefore, it is vitally important to create structures and shared expectations for peer observation at the outset. It may also be helpful to provide practice in observation. As mentioned previously, such practice might begin through the use of video material from classrooms outside the school.

A pair of teachers can carry out open-ended observations in each of their classrooms. The purpose is not only to practice describing what they see without making evaluative statements, but also to examine the commonalities and differences in what each teacher observes.

- The two teachers meet prior to the observation period and the teacher who will be observed describes what will be happening in the classroom.
- The observer tries to capture in as much detail as possible what occurs during the observation period, perhaps scripting what is said by the teacher and students.
- In a debriefing session, the observer reconstructs what occurred, drawing upon the notes taken during the observation period. The teacher who was observed listens, making note of details that escaped his or her notice and adding additional observations.
- The observed teacher responds to the comments of the observer, distinguishing the commonalities and differences in the observations that each teacher made. Both the observer and the observed teacher avoid making

In her book, *In Schools We Trust*, principal Deborah Meier writes about the challenges of establishing peer observation as part of the staff's professional learning. Although the teaching cadre was small and close-knit, the teachers were nervous both about being observed and about observing. People were afraid of jeopardizing positive relationships by offering commentary on each other's practices. The teachers had to learn to give and get feedback without taking things personally.

value judgments or subjective interpretations, focusing instead on a neutral description of what was seen and heard.

Peer observation is most effective, however, if it is situated within a professional learning community's ongoing inquiry into specific aspects of teaching. In that context, both the observer and the teacher being observed share a common goal and the observation exercise becomes an opportunity to learn from each other. The observer is not a critic, but a co-teacher who may be able to offer a different perspective and constructive feedback.

Into the Classroom

A group of high school English teachers could work to enhance their students' writing through a writing workshop and their specific focus might be conferences with student writers. They might spend time making observations in each other's classrooms with the following question in mind: "What evidence do I observe that students are using feedback from instructor and peer conferences as they make useful revision and editing decisions?"

Teachers in a professional learning community might find themselves working on different aspects of a shared focus. In such a situation, each teacher may structure the observations differently, developing an individual focus question for the observer. For example, individuals within a group of teachers working to improve problem solving in mathematics could develop a focus on improving their demonstration lessons. In this case, the focus question might be: "To what extent do my explanations and questions result in active student participation and application of new concepts?" Individuals interested in developing more effective concrete or visual models might develop a focus question such as: "What evidence do you see that students' use of visual or concrete models enhances problem solving?" Teachers intent on enhancing students' understanding of the language of mathematics might explore the focus question: "What evidence do you see that students are acquiring mathematical language and using it appropriately?" Focus questions related to students' independent application of problem-solving strategies might be: "What evidence do you see of students' application of problem-solving strategies when they are working independently? Do some students need more support?"

Guidelines for Peer Observation

Regardless of the focus of peer observation, the process should have a predictable structure that is well understood by all participants. The following guidelines can be adapted for specific situations.

- **Before the Visit**
  The teachers meet and discuss the purpose(s) of the observation and agree upon a time frame and the nature of the observations. The person to be observed describes what will be happening in the classroom and identifies a focusing question. The teachers should decide, as well, how the visitor will behave in the classroom so as to minimize disruption, for example, will the visitor stand or sit in a designated spot or circulate quietly throughout the room? Appropriate behavior will depend upon the nature of the learning experiences during the visit.

- **During the Visit**

  The observer makes notes that are descriptive rather than interpretive or judgmental. The observer may also jot down questions that occur to him or her while observing interactions in the classroom.

- **After the Visit**

  During a debriefing session, the observer shares notes related to the focus of observation. The most helpful stance is that of a "second pair of eyes" that may capture details missed by the person doing the teaching. The observer may pose a question such as: "How did you feel about the lesson?" The person observed can share his or her perceptions and the observer might point to evidence from the notes that either supports or contradicts those perceptions. The observer might also ask clarifying questions, make summary notes, or introduce questions that arose during observation. The pair may explore possibilities for changes in professional practices that might evolve from the insights gained through the observations and subsequent discussion.

Once teachers have gained experience with peer observation and have developed highly trusting and supportive relationships, they may draw upon each other's expertise to solve specific problems in the classroom. For example, a teacher might be having difficulty managing the behavior of a small group or the class as a whole and might seek a peer's assistance in finding more effective ways to redirect the attention of students. Or, a teacher who is puzzled about why a previously successful practice does not seem to be engaging a particular group of students might ask a colleague to help identify what is going wrong.

Such problem solving centred on areas of difficulty is feasible only when both colleagues understand it as a process of working together to discover and construct new understandings. Teachers will risk allowing peers to become aware of areas of weakness when a culture of trust and mutual support has become well established in the school.

SCENARIO

Two Grade 4 teachers, Craig and Mark, were members of a professional learning community focused on improving teaching practices in elementary science. In the course of the group's discussions, they discovered that they were both struggling with ways to plan and support students' small group investigations. Each teacher wanted students to engage in experiences that captured the students' natural curiosity but that also supported the development of students' skills in questioning, observing, recording observations, and analyzing results.

Craig had more experience teaching Grade 4 science compared to Mark, and he shared some of the ways by which he had supported students' inquiries. Mark was curious about how successful investigations actually worked in Craig's classroom. Craig was eager to receive feedback from another teacher on his efforts. The two agreed to approach the principal to arrange a classroom visit, which the principal was more than willing to do by covering Mark's classroom herself on an afternoon when Craig taught science for an hour and then was free during the following hour while his students spent time with a specialist teacher.

The week before the visit, Craig and Mark met to plan the observation session. They agreed that the observation would focus on how Craig supported the student's application of the skills of questioning, making observations, and recording data as they completed investigations using batteries and light bulbs.

...teaching, like parenting, involves acts of judgment that cut close to who we are, whether we are "good people" as well as whether we are competent people. Even with advance warning, it's hard to hide much. And the most neutral feedback ("this is what I saw") can hurt: a documentary film, after all, is not without its point of view. If the feedback hurts too much, we're going to build barriers that cut off the view. Meier, 2002, p. 66

Craig explained to his students that he would be conducting a mini-lesson to review with students what they had already learned about these skills and to remind them to apply them in the new activity. He told students he would circulate among the groups for the rest of the hour and Mark would be free to observe and interact with the students.

During the visit, Mark made notes on all aspects of the lesson: both the teacher instruction as well as student small group activities. He recorded student comments that reflected differing levels of sophistication in questioning and observation. He jotted down questions of his own to ask Craig in the debriefing session.

In the discussion of Mark's notes during the debriefing session, Craig commented that he had been unaware that his mini-lesson at the beginning of the observation period had lasted 20 minutes when he had intended to complete this mini-lesson in only 10 minutes! Both teachers discussed how important it is to keep these introductory min-lessons brief and tightly focused so that students have maximum time to conduct an investigation.

Mark commented that the students appeared very absorbed and task-focused and he asked Craig what prior instruction had occurred to develop this attentiveness to the task. Craig said he was pleased with how the students had worked and he shared what he had done earlier in the year.

Mark talked about a group of students who appeared to be struggling and Craig commented that he had to find a way to devote more time to that group or to develop additional supports for them. Mark, who had experience as a resource teacher, commented that it seemed to him that the students were having trouble reading and interpreting the procedural instructions for conducting the investigation, so perhaps they could benefit from less complex language and more graphics. The two peers continued their discussion in that vein. At the end of the debriefing hour, Mark asked if Craig would be willing to visit his classroom to observe a similar investigation.

The two teachers brought their questions about effective, focused mini-lessons and support for struggling readers in science back to the larger professional learning community and the group agreed to devote attention to these questions as part of their larger inquiry focus.

Lesson Study: Designing and Teaching a Focused Lesson

Lesson study has been a central focus for teacher professional development in Japan for two centuries and it has been adapted by a wide variety of districts and schools in North America. In Japan, the teaching day is designed to provide scheduled time both for classroom contact with students and for the teachers' own professional development. In North America, in contrast, the teacher's time is devoted primarily to instruction in the classroom. Therefore, while lesson study is an integral aspect of teachers' work in Japan, it is more difficult to implement in North American classrooms. Where lesson study has been successfully implemented, principals have played a key role through creative scheduling and the deployment of specialist teachers and other professionals to provide meaningful instruction for students while teachers are engaged in lesson study planning, observation, and discussion sessions.

Lesson study involves seven recursive steps as shown in the list and the cycle diagram on the following page.

1. Definition of a teaching problem
2. Collaborative design of a lesson or teaching unit to address the problem
3. Group observation of one teacher teaching the lesson or unit
4. Debriefing focused on the impact on student learning
5. Redesign of the lesson based on the evidence collected
6. Teaching the revised lesson to a different group of students
7. Further reflection and discussion

Small Group Lesson Study

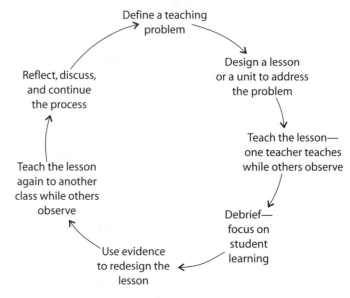

A research lesson is not a demonstration lesson that showcases a particular teacher or approach. Nor is it a formal report of research findings, presented by the teacher as if at a professional meeting. Instead, a teacher or lesson study group shares research findings in the form of a research lesson so that the participants can analyze the research data during the post-lesson discussion. Watanabe, 2002, p. 37

As noted above, the focus of evaluating the success of the lesson is always in terms of student learning. Therefore, this type of activity is a powerful means of keeping students in the forefront as the central focus of teacher professional development. Lesson study also creates a context within which teachers can try out new practices in collaboration with peers—thus making it more likely that they will be successful in making complex changes in their teaching practices.

How a Lesson Study Unfolds

The focus of a lesson study evolves through the goal-setting process that frames the work of the professional learning community. Considering the following kinds of questions can help a group define the teaching problem that they wish to address:

- What do we want for our students? What do we want them to have accomplished by the time they leave us?
- Where are the gaps between what we aspire toward and what our students are achieving?
- What area of need will provide the focus for our lesson study?
- What, specifically, do we wish our lesson(s) to accomplish? What is our ultimate goal?

A small lesson development group (no more than three or four people) then designs a lesson or, in all likelihood, a series of lessons to accomplish the goal, drawing upon curriculum guides and other professional resources. The lesson study group as a whole should decide upon a consistent format for the lesson or unit plan. This format may be one already used in the school or district or one devised by the group itself. Next, someone within the lesson design group must volunteer to teach the lesson with the entire lesson study group as observers.

The group should also agree upon a structure for the observations and the follow-up debriefing session. A detailed lesson study protocol developed by the Lesson Study Research Group at Teachers College/Columbia University (www.tc.edu/centers/lessonstudy) is available for download. The overall framework for observation is similar to paired peer observation in that there are tasks before, during, and after the lesson.

- **Before the Lesson**
  The group reviews their shared focus and the planning group distributes copies of the lesson plan to all observers. The group conducting the observation may wish to decide in advance the nature of each observer's role. For example, one observer could focus on teacher interactions and others might focus on the interactions within particular groups of students. Having the students wear name tags will facilitate note-taking and later discussion.
- **During the Lesson**
  Observers try to be as unobtrusive as possible so that the lesson proceeds in as natural a way as is feasible given a number of additional people in the room. Observers follow along with the lesson plan, making notes about the agreed-upon area of observation. Observers function as researchers, collecting data that will be interpreted later in the debriefing session.
- **After the Lesson**
  The debriefing session is the most important part of the lesson study. There should be time for observers to review their notes and to reflect upon what they have observed. Although one teacher has taught the lesson, all those involved in the design should receive feedback on the lesson.

  The designers begin the discussion by sharing their perceptions about how the lesson went and what could be changed. Then they invite feedback from observers, keeping the focus on the goal of the lesson. Observers can set a supportive tone by highlighting the positive aspects of the lesson at the outset. The comments should not focus on the teacher's style or the success or failure of the lesson, but on data relevant to the goal. The observers may ask clarifying questions and offer constructive feedback. For example, a teacher might comment, "I noticed that three of the six students I observed did not seem to be able to follow the instructions. They kept asking other students what they were supposed to do." Observers should take turns offering one or two points and the designers should refrain from immediate response to specific comments. Rather, they should consider and reflect upon all the feedback before offering their perceptions and asking questions.

  The debriefing session should result in insights into the strengths and weaknesses of the lesson design, as well as suggestions for improvement. The lesson design group can use the feedback to redesign the lesson and then teach it again in a different classroom with the lesson study group as a whole as observers.

It can be extremely helpful to a lesson study group to invite professionals from outside the school to offer their expertise and insights into lesson design. These "knowledgeable others" might be district consultants, university faculty members, or representatives from provincial or state educational authorities. These professionals can offer their expertise not only as observers but also as consultants during the lesson design process. This outside perspective can greatly enrich the discussions and enhance learning as experts share the most recent research and help expand teachers' knowledge of current theories and practices.

Web 2.0—Tapping into Expertise Through Videoconferencing

Technology may help to facilitate the use of outside consultants as part of lesson study. It may be impractical for professionals with relevant expertise to meet face-to-face with teacher groups at the school level, but teacher groups and outside professionals may be able to connect through videoconferencing, and perhaps provide support to more than one group by this means. For example, teachers from several elementary schools who are working on math lessons could benefit from a videoconference with a professor of mathematics education from a university located at a considerable distance from the schools. Schools may be able to arrange videoconferences through district or provincial/state technology departments or through a university's distance learning services.

SCENARIO

Five Grade 1 teachers in a large elementary school had formed a professional learning community with a focus on improving their teaching of mathematics. Evidence from classroom assessments and provincial testing had shown that many students were not achieving grade-level outcomes/standards in mathematical problem solving. The Grade 1 teachers shared an interest in giving more emphasis to problem solving by engaging students in more active and exploratory learning experiences. They had concerns, however, about how to ensure that all children grasped the mathematical concepts and skills within such teaching environments.

After several months of reading, discussion, and examination of mathematics curriculum documents, the teachers decided that it would be worthwhile to engage in a lesson study process. Their principal was able to tap into district-level professional development funding to hire substitute teachers to support their work.

Two of the teachers, Sarita and Diane, volunteered to develop a lesson that Sarita would teach while the four other teachers acted as observers. Sarita had already strengthened her attention to the development of problem solving strategies and was interested in seeing how well students could apply what they had been learning. The designers developed a lesson that described in more detail the steps outlined on the following page.

1. In an opening whole-group lesson, the teacher worked through a problem with the children. She named the strategies that she and the children used and she recorded on chart paper the steps that she used in deciding how to solve the problem.
2. Then each of the students, who were seated at tables in small groups of four, was given a problem to solve. On each table the teacher placed manipulative materials that students could use as needed and a recording form on which to document their thinking. The form was appropriate for Grade 1 students who have limited writing skills because it provided ways to record ideas by checking boxes, drawing pictures, or using simple words. Students in each group were assigned the roles of leader and recorder. As the children worked on their problems, the teacher circulated and supported their learning by answering questions and providing prompts as necessary.
3. The final part of the lesson involved whole-group debriefing and sharing.

Before the observation of Sarita teaching the lesson took place, the teachers met and discussed the lesson plan. They assigned each observer a different role: one observer focused on the teacher's talk and actions, while each of the three other teachers focused on two tables of students, making observations on the students' application of the problem-solving strategies they had been taught and their use of the materials provided. The observation session took place and the teachers met later that day to debrief.

Sarita opened the debriefing session by saying that she thought that the lesson had gone well, but that both she and Maria realized that many of the students found the recording form too difficult to use. Nonetheless, the children had remained engaged and had demonstrated growing ability to apply a range of mathematical problem-solving strategies. The observers who had been assigned to student tables provided detailed observations on how well each group had managed and they commented on the strengths and needs of specific children within the groups. Two of the observers noticed that students had difficulties with the recording form. However, the other observer commented that the students at the two tables that she had observed seemed to handle the form with no difficulty.

Sarita asked the group how well they thought her instruction at the beginning had prepared the students for the small-group learning. Everyone agreed that the short lesson at the outset had been very effective. The discussion continued with further sharing of observations and questions.

At the end of the session, Sarita and Maria volunteered to revise the lesson, making small changes and redesigning the recording form. Testing out the revisions, Maria taught the lesson in her classroom and the group again observed the lesson. As a result of the discussions that had taken place during the lesson study, the members of the professional learning community agreed that they would continue to work on mathematical problem solving, placing particular emphasis on how to support those children who were not yet applying the strategies that they had been taught previously, as well as on those children who were ready for greater challenges.

Redesigning Lessons

Redesigning lessons is an integral part of the recursive process of lesson study. Redesigning lessons can also be a productive activity on its own. Teachers may have developed practices that have addressed the needs of students quite well, but changes in the student population or revised curriculum documents may require that teachers adopt different ways of teaching. It can be extremely beneficial for teachers to begin with what they know by revising lessons that have been successful in the past.

For example, as classrooms have become more diverse, teachers face the challenge of responding to a wider range of student needs. Teachers can meet these needs more effectively by redesigning lessons to make them more open-ended. Such lessons engage students in a common experience but provide opportunities for multiple forms of response at different levels of complexity and in different response modes. In terms of assessment, students are able to demonstrate their learning in a variety of ways using different types of evidence. A group of teachers engaged in redesigning existing lessons might structure the process as follows:

1. Develop criteria for open-ended lessons.
2. Choose an existing lesson and determine how it meets the criteria and how it falls short.
3. Discuss ways in which the lesson could be made more open-ended. Consider questions such as:
   • What is the expected outcome of this lesson?
   • In what diverse ways can students achieve this outcome?
   • What do we know about the students that can help us design a lesson in which all students can engage and experience success?
   • How can we build in more choice for students?
   • How can we group students to maximize success?
   • Where in the lesson are there options for more than one form of response?
   • How can we incorporate additional resources (e.g., multi-leveled books, manipulative materials in mathematics, visual representations, etc.) that will help more children to experience success?
   • How can we provide a range of assessment options so that students can use different types of evidence to demonstrate their learning?
4. Redesign the lesson and ask members of the group to try it out in their classrooms.
5. Rejoin the group for reflection, discussion, and further revision.

SCENARIO

A group of seven Grades 5 and 6 teachers had been working collaboratively for two years, focusing primarily on improving teaching in English language arts. At a session early in November, just before report card time, two Grade 6 teachers, Cheryl and Dan, dropped into their chairs and slammed a large binder down on the table. "Can you believe the size of this guide for health? They've added even more to what we've already been teaching! How can we adequately address all that content when we are already working flat out trying to improve literacy and numeracy?"

"Well," replied Rebecca, a Grade 5 teacher new to the school who was in her second year of teaching, "I know how you feel. Last year I was at another school that was piloting that new program. I was a first year teacher and was developing PowerPoint presentations and designing activities for every bit of the health content. I was just about in tears one day when my principal sat down with me and asked, 'Why are you doing all the work? Why can't you involve the students more?' She helped me figure out ways to involve the students in research so that small groups became experts on specific topics."

"I can see how that kind of research would also address what we've been trying to do to improve literacy," said Cheryl. "We've been working on content reading and writing. Let's give the health curriculum a go!"

After examining the curriculum documents, the Grade 6 teachers decided that they would begin by redesigning the section on disease prevention. They created a unit in which students worked in triads to become experts on how to prevent a range of illnesses. The students gathered information from a variety of sources and then assumed responsibility for teaching their peers about the disease on which they had become an expert. The teachers encouraged students to use participatory activities and multimedia in their teaching sessions, and they built in classroom assessment processes through which children considered the question, "What makes a good lesson?"

Each of the Grade 6 teachers implemented the three-week unit in their classrooms. In a debriefing session afterwards, the teachers were excited about how much the students had learned, not only about the health content, but also about how to use language and literacy for learning. The teachers also reflected on the changes in their practices: instead of spending prep time and evenings developing PowerPoint slides and then delivering health lessons, the teachers were much more actively engaged in supporting the students' self-directed learning, offering focused instruction to the class, small groups, and individuals as needed. Based on the success of the unit, the teachers decided to redesign other sections of the health curriculum, building upon what they had learned about the specific needs and interests of their students.

If you've just begun to dip your toes into the digital waters, work with your peers to create a collaborative writing wiki. Wikis are editable Web sites and, like blogs, they require little technical skill to master. Wiki toolbars look just like those in common word-processing programs; when you're finished saving contributions to a wiki page, your work is automatically posted online.
Ferriter, 2009, p. 37

🌎🌎🌎 Web 2.0—Online Lesson Design

Collaborative lesson design can extend beyond the school when teachers are willing to post draft lessons and invite responses and input from individuals and groups from other schools. When teachers explore different ways in which to teach a specific concept or skill, they can create a cross-school collection of lesson and unit plans that each school-based group can discuss and critique. Then all those participating can share the results of their conversations electronically, thus gaining the benefit of many different perspectives. Such collaborations may lead to the design of lesson and unit plans that incorporate the best of everyone's ideas. Wikis are particularly helpful tools for collaborative lesson design because they allow participants to make changes easily to texts. As noted earlier, a free wiki platform is available at this website: http://pbworks.com/academic.wiki

Learning Through Reflection

All of the approaches to rethinking teaching practices described in this chapter involve groups of professionals reflecting critically on their own work. Through this type of reflection, teachers can become more alert to what is going on in their own classrooms and they can learn from each other's best practices. Ongoing inquiry into teaching is a powerful form of support that teachers can draw upon when they are grappling with the complexities inherent in their profession. Ongoing inquiry is also a means of enhancing creative problem solving and celebrating individual and group accomplishments.

Chapter 6 explores further possibilities for collaborative planning and instruction. It offers a number of suggestions for ways in which teachers can work together over extended time frames, further strengthening their professional learning communities and establishing a culture of collaboration within their school.

Extended Collaborations

Chapter 5 presents a number of suggestions for ways in which teachers can collaborate effectively in planning and teaching. Once teachers have developed positive and mutually beneficial working relationships, they can extend that collaboration through longer term undertakings, such as joint planning, co-teaching, development of common assessments, and classroom inquiry/action research. Such practices help to shift a school from a culture of isolation to a culture in which collaboration is the norm, rather than the exception.

Joint Planning

Joint planning is, in essence, a form of team teaching that does not involve actually working together in a classroom. Such planning can be a step on the way to collaborative teaching or it can be a valuable activity on its own. Joint planning provides opportunities for teachers to discuss how best to meet outcomes/standards and to share expertise, teaching ideas, and resources so that all classes benefit from the collective efforts of several teachers. Teachers can meet in groups according to grade level or subject area and design and teach the same material. Additionally, teachers of different subjects at the middle or high school level can design and teach cross-disciplinary units.

Whatever the teacher grouping structure that is developed, joint planning contributes to the development of more coherent and consistent programs for students. Robert Marzano (2003) carried out a meta-analysis of school achievement and ranked "a guaranteed and viable curriculum" as having the most impact on student learning, but he commented that "the notion of a coherent, implemented curriculum is a myth" (p. 23). While it is important that individual teachers design their classroom programs to ensure that all students meet the mandated outcomes/standards, those individual efforts need to result in a coherent whole for students.

A large body of research documents indicate that this is far from the case in many schools. In an analysis of a series of studies related to how curriculum is enacted across the grade levels, Schmoker (2006) concluded that "curriculum chaos continues to be among the best-kept secrets in education" (p. 37). These studies consistently show that redundancy and inconsistency exist at every grade level; also, the curriculum that many students actually experience is fragmented and poorly aligned with outcomes/standards. The message is clear: teachers need to "be on the same page" in terms of planning, or student achievement will suffer.

Before undertaking joint planning, a professional learning community should have engaged in reading, discussion, and other joint work that has

Curriculum mapping is an invaluable tool that can help schools clean their closets…. Teachers create individual curriculum maps that identify by calendar months the topics, skills, and assessments they are addressing. They then analyze individual maps through the grades and course to assess vertical articulation and alignment to academic standards.
Jacobs, 2004, p. vi

helped them to reach a common understanding of teaching philosophy, goals, and best practices. If a group has not had honest exchanges about differences in beliefs and practices and has not worked through those differences, the members will find it difficult, if not impossible, to agree upon the design of a teaching plan.

Web 2.0—Joint Planning Beyond the School

Teachers in small schools with only one teacher per grade or subject area can engage in joint planning or the development of common assessments online, perhaps remotely by joining a professional learning community in a larger school or by developing an online community among several small schools. Participants can exchange draft teaching plans electronically and, if the technology is available, the group can have periodic videoconferences to discuss work-in-progress.

Grade-Level or Subject Area Planning

When professional learning communities are formed according to grade level or subject area, the members already share much in common in terms of the curriculum, student achievement targets, and the nature of their teaching assignments. While each teacher's class will feature individual characteristics, there should be much that is similar about the classroom contexts.

The joint planning process will evolve differently, however, depending upon the prior experiences of the group members. For example, if the group members have all taught the grade level or subject area for several years, each teacher will have many teaching ideas and resources to contribute. Nonetheless, each member must also be open to the ideas and resources of others. The members of the group need to believe that their collaborative planning efforts will enhance their individual practices. If the teachers have less experience in terms of the grade level or subject area, they will have fewer classroom-tested ideas to contribute at the outset. However, they can share the workload required to prepare to teach a new grade level or subject. When the group includes a combination of experienced and less experienced teachers, both categories of teachers can benefit from the synthesis of tested practices and fresh perspectives.

A Framework for Joint Planning

The process outlined below provides a flexible framework for joint planning that can be adapted in response to specific needs, interests, and logistical issues. The professional learning group must agree upon a format for the plan and a means of recording and organizing information during the planning process. A clear and fair distribution of the required tasks among group members will contribute to harmony and efficiency.

1. **Discuss and agree upon goals for student learning**: What do teachers want their students to know and be able to do as a result of engagement in these learning experiences? Teachers should review provincial/state, district, and local outcomes/standards as well as school and classroom data to determine appropriate achievement targets.

2. **Define the needs of students**: What do we know about the learners in each of our classrooms? Each teacher identifies issues that must be addressed in planning, for example, classrooms in which many learners struggle with literacy, groups of students that are difficult to handle from a disciplinary perspective, classes with many high achievers, or classrooms with many learners who have special needs requiring accommodations. The joint plan will have to be sufficiently flexible and inclusive to address the specifics of each teaching context.

3. **Brainstorm ideas**: What types of learning experiences will contribute to student achievement of these outcomes? How have we taught this topic before? What new ideas do we have? This is the time for everyone to explore, to consider a broad range of possibilities, sharing their prior experiences and gathering new ideas. The group might refer to curriculum guides and professional resources for additional suggestions related to the evolving plan.

4. **Cull and expand**: Which of the many ideas seem to have the greatest potential? How can we expand upon and become more specific about the ideas that we choose? In this part of the process, the group begins to clarify and sharpen their goals, making decisions about the types of learning experiences to include and the materials and resources they will need. Group members can share relevant individual lesson plans and descriptions of activities.

5. **Pool resources:** What resources do we already have in our classrooms and in the school to support these learning experiences? What additional resources do we need to find or acquire? In this part of the process, teachers survey the resources in their classrooms and in the school to determine what is available to support the teaching plan. The group should consider both print and online resources and tap into services such as curriculum resource libraries or other centralized distribution systems within school districts.

6. **Construct the plan:** How will we transform our ideas into a coherent and organized plan? The group will need to make final decisions about the content and sequence of learning experiences, assessment, individual lessons, and materials. It is helpful if a small writing team consisting of two or three people assumes responsibility for pulling the ideas together for consideration by the whole group.

7. **Teach and reflect:** As each teacher implements the plan in the classroom, the group can meet periodically to discuss how the plan is evolving. Teachers can share what is going well and describe revisions that they have made based on their students' responses. After all the teachers have worked through the plan in their classrooms, the group can attend a final session to reflect on the plan's strengths and weaknesses and to make further revisions to be incorporated when they use the plan with future classes.

After a professional learning community gains some experience planning together, they may progress to the development of semester- or year-long plans. This approach has the advantage of ensuring that all outcomes are addressed and that the program is balanced and varied. Such planning helps when schools are making decisions about the purchase of resources, since needs are planned for and anticipated in advance. Teachers can revisit and improve these year-long plans over time, creating rich, coherent, and well-supported learning experiences for all students across multiple classrooms.

Cross-Disciplinary Planning

When teachers from several disciplines plan together within a professional learning community, they have opportunities to explore the connections across subject areas, thus helping students to understand the interrelationships among the different areas of the curriculum that they are studying. While the benefits of interdisciplinary teaching are self-evident in terms of greater opportunities for students to see the connections across disciplines, there are persistent concerns about diluting the individual subject disciplines through curriculum integration. Therefore, it is crucial that a professional learning community that is contemplating cross-disciplinary planning spend time at the outset learning about each of the subject areas and identifying related outcomes/standards, content, skills, and processes. Working from a clear conception of what is expected in terms of student learning within each subject area is the most effective way to ensure the integrity of the disciplines, while also maximizing possibilities for integration.

For an example of cross-disciplinary planning in action, see pages 91–93 in *Yes, but…if they like it, they'll learn it!* (Church, Baskwill, and Swain, 2007).

Interdisciplinary Teaching

In a 1995 position statement on interdisciplinary curriculum, the major national subject-matter organizations—the National Council of Teachers of Mathematics, the National Council of Teachers of English, the International Reading Association, the National Science Teachers Association, the National Council for Social Studies, the Speech Communication Association, and the Council for Elementary Science International—noted:

> Recent calls for educational reform focus on the need for curricula emphasizing conceptual learning that is integrated across traditional subject areas. Basic to this effort is the belief that educational experiences are more authentic and of greater value to students when the curricula reflect real life, which is multifaceted—rather than being compartmentalized into neat subject-matter packages. Interdisciplinary instruction capitalizes on natural and logical connections that cut across content areas and is organized around questions, themes, problems, or projects rather than along traditional subject-matter boundaries. Such instruction is likely to be responsive to children's curiosity and questions about real life and to result in productive learning and positive attitudes toward school and teachers.
>
> The participating organizations believe that educational experiences should help develop children's natural curiosity and their inclination to construct meaning. A focus on relationships across disciplines should encourage creative problem solving and decision making because it makes available to students the perspectives, knowledge, and data-gathering skills of all the disciplines. Such an instructional process should also encourage children to interact with others in a learning community where diversity of thought and culture is valued. (NCTE, 2009)

The website of Edutopia (www.edutopia.org), an educational foundation devoted to highlighting what works in public education, provides many examples of integrated studies, project-based learning, and other forms of collaboration.

There are a number of different models for integrating planning and instruction across two or more subjects. The list that follows is ordered according to a model that requires the least collaboration to one that will succeed only if teachers are committed to working together, co-creating learning experiences with their students.

- Correlate content and learning processes across subjects, for example, social studies teachers and English language arts teachers might teach the history and literature of the same era in their respective classrooms, or both might work with primary sources at the same time, addressing social studies and English language arts outcomes.
- Integrate skills across disciplines, for example, address literacy in all subject areas.
- Focus on one subject and integrate the skills and content from other subjects, for example, in a science classroom teach content reading and writing (language arts), explore the impact of science on society (social studies), and incorporate scientific drawing (visual arts).
- Organize lessons around a theme (environmental issues, the future, change, survival, families) or an inquiry question (How can we sustain the economy and the environment in our community? What are the relationships between constancy and change?)
- Organize the teaching of several subjects around a long-term project, for example, a community study or service learning initiative in which students receive credit for providing service to the community.

Correlate content and learning across subjects	Integrate skills across disciplines	Focus on one subject and integrate the skills and content of other subjects	Organize lessons around a theme	Organize the teaching of several subjects around a long-term project

The process for cross-disciplinary planning is similar to the one outlined earlier for same-grade level or subject-area planning, but with some additional steps. The process is intended for a group of teachers from different subject areas who are working with the same group of students.

1. **Decide upon a focus** (theme, inquiry question, or project), ensuring that it is broad enough to allow meaningful exploration in all disciplines represented by teachers in the group. Take time to share insights into the focus from the perspective of each discipline.
2. **Examine outcomes from each discipline:** Having agreed upon a focus, each teacher needs to determine which outcomes/standards can best be addressed through the unit. As a group, teachers can then look for commonalities in the outcomes across disciplines as well as identify subject-specific outcomes that will be the sole responsibility of that subject-area teacher.

3. **Describe the needs and interests of learners:** Think about and discuss what teachers know about the learners that will influence planning. Where are students in relationship to achievement of the outcomes? What are students' needs in terms of skills development? How can the plan be structured to respond to students' interests and strengths? What kinds of learning experiences seem best suited to this group of students?

4. **Brainstorm ideas:** The brainstorming might begin with each teacher recording ideas for how the unit focus could be explored in a subject area in order to support students' achievement of the outcomes. The brainstorm should be as open and exploratory as possible, including questions, topics, learning experiences, assessments, and resources (both print and online media as well as human resources). The group can then combine their ideas in a larger brainstorming session using a web or bicycle wheel graphic organizer (in which the organizing focus appears in the centre and each subject appears on a line or spoke).

5. **Organize and sequence:** Moving from brainstorming to an organized plan requires that each teacher and the group as a whole conceptualize a sequence for exploring the focus in the most coherent way. This might involve the generation of questions or subcategories within the larger focus. These can be recorded in a matrix or a chart with each subject area across the top, as shown in the example on the following page. (A blank version of this chart is included as a blackline master at the back of this book.) The example shows how a group of teachers began to work with subquestions and identified ways to explore the questions in each discipline. The next organizational step would be to look across the ideas and decide what to do when in each individual discipline and how to coordinate the exploration across the classrooms. For example, the students could read historical fiction from World War II in English language arts, examine primary sources and nonfiction accounts in social studies, and explore visual representations from the World War II era in art class.

6. **Pool resources:** The group must determine what resources are available to support the unit and what additional materials they will need to acquire.

7. **Develop lesson plans:** Teachers can work individually and collaboratively to generate specific lesson plans for each of the classrooms involved. These lessons should be designed so students' experiences in each classroom are connected and coherent. The idea is to implement one unit with some outcomes and experiences that are common to all disciplines, along with some subject-specific outcomes.

8. **Finalize and construct the plan:** The final plan will be a document that all teachers can work from, implementing different aspects as outlined in the plan.

9. **Teach and reflect:** During the implementation of a cross-disciplinary plan, it is extremely important that the professional learning community meet regularly to discuss how implementation of the plan is progressing in each classroom. Ongoing communication will facilitate timely revisions as teachers and students work through the plan together. With such units there are often unexpected, but very fruitful, paths of inquiry that emerge as the topic is explored. The plan and the teachers implementing it need to be flexible enough to respond to these opportunities to enrich

Cross-Disciplinary Planning

Topic or Large Inquiry Question: _How do humans survive?_ [This example shows the beginning ideas recorded by a group of teachers planning an inquiry unit together. Each teacher jotted down ideas for ways in which questions could be explored in a discipline; the next step would be to organize the ideas in a sequence of connected experiences and decide who would do what.]

Subquestions or Subcategories	English Language Arts	Social Studies	Math	Science	Art
What kinds of challenges do people face?	Read fiction and non-fiction about individuals and groups; interview family or community members about challenges; write about one's own challenges	Create a simulation of settlers in a new environment: What do they need to do to survive? Examine primary sources from similar situations, e.g., early settlers of North America	Learn how probability and statistics help to document and predict human survival	Investigate human biology and responses to environmental challenges, e.g., protective factors, fight or flight, adaptation to the environment, etc.	Create representations in response to reading and activities in other disciplines; respond to examples of artists' responses to challenges
How have different groups throughout history survived?	Read historical fiction and nonfiction; explore media from other eras; conduct individual inquiry projects re. specific groups	Examine the history of survival of different cultural groups; investigate students' own family histories of survival	Could possibly do something with stats here but don't want to force it	Examine how technology has influenced human survival	Investigate how art contributes to the survival of cultures
How do people survive wars?	Read first-person accounts, biographies and fiction related to war; use drama to represent survival situations; explore how human relationships impact survival	Examine the history of war from a human perspective: Who survives and who doesn't? What kinds of sacrifices have people made?	Examine the story of different wars told through statistics; how are statistics used as propaganda?		
What are the greatest challenges to human survival today?	Carry out small group inquiry projects related to issues such as climate change, poverty, and war	Research for inquiry projects could be done in both English and social studies classes	How are data (represented in different ways such as graphs or charts) used to support contrasting positions on controversial issues?	Focus on the science of climate change	Students construct visual representations to express their thoughts and feelings about issues that impact their futures

the learning. At the conclusion of the unit, students and teachers can evaluate the plan critically to determine what changes could be made to improve it in the future.

Developing Common Assessments

Although the development of common assessments is an integral part of joint planning, in this age of accountability it can also become a primary focus for a professional learning community outside the context of larger joint planning efforts. If teachers have not engaged in professional learning related to quality classroom assessment, including the development of clear learning targets or goals, as discussed in Chapter 3, designing assessments together is unlikely to lead to changes in practices or improvements in student achievement and may, instead, simply create consistency, rather than higher-quality student assessment. For example, teachers unfamiliar with a broad range of sources of assessment information may simply work together to construct common tests that they will all use rather than consider how to use a repertoire of classroom assessment practices more effectively to guide instruction and to promote student learning.

Stiggins and DuFour (2009) advocate the development of common formative assessments—those that provide information to guide each student's learning journey as well as the teacher's instructional decision making—within school-based professional learning communities for three purposes:

1. To identify areas of the curriculum that need strengthening or more focus because many students are not reaching learning targets
2. To identify individual and collective strengths and weaknesses in teaching practices
3. To identify individual students who need additional support or alternative interventions to enable them to be successful

Common assessments can establish where each student is now in the learning progression and where students are collectively across classrooms, thus serving the information needs of both teachers and students.
Stiggins and DuFour, 2009, p. 643

By focusing on the development of common assessments, teachers of the same grade or subject who have formed a professional learning community can work collectively to gather information that provides a picture of how all students in that grade or subject are progressing. The teachers can share their expertise and insights in making decisions about how to change instruction to enhance student success. Teachers who design common classroom assessments have a greater need to clarify learning targets than teachers who are working alone. Through the collective examination of standards/outcomes and discussion regarding their meaning and implications for teaching (see Chapter 3), teachers develop a shared understanding and consistent interpretation of the goals for student learning. For the development of common assessments to function as a useful tool for improving student learning, professional learning communities must do the following:

- Clarify learning goals/targets (see Chapter 3 for suggestions).
- Expand knowledge of best practices in classroom assessment.
- Discuss how best to assess each learning target, identifying multiple sources of information.

- Determine the range and amount of information to be gathered in order to be confident that it represents a true picture of student learning.
- Design assessments and begin to implement them in classrooms.
- Bring data to professional learning community meetings and work together to analyze and interpret the data, and then discuss implications for instruction (see Chapter 4 for suggestions related to examining student work); consider how to communicate the findings most clearly to students, parents/guardians, and administrators.
- Act upon the information by providing feedback to students and making changes in instruction.
- Continue refining assessments and instruction individually and as a group.

As the list above demonstrates, the process of developing common assessments involves an examination of teachers' beliefs, goals, assumptions, knowledge, and current assessment practices. By sharing their expertise and becoming better informed about assessment practices, teachers can improve the quality of their classroom assessments. Furthermore, they will be able to speak about student learning with the same voice when communicating with family members, administrators, and the community at large.

Co-teaching

Any teacher who has had the experience of teaching with another colleague knows that it can be a source of great mutual support, shared expertise, and positive energy. Research shows that co-teaching leads to a more positive work climate, increased teacher job satisfaction, improved communication with parents/guardians, and enhanced student achievement. Co-teaching can also be a teacher's worst nightmare, however, if partners are not well-matched or if insufficient attention has been paid to the details of how the teaming will work. With a team larger than two, there is an even greater need for clear parameters.

When co-teaching evolves as a result of the ongoing interactions of a professional learning community, it is likely that team members will have worked together long enough to have a strong basis from which to develop well-functioning co-teaching arrangements. This type of collaboration moves the work of the professional learning community directly into the classroom and has the potential to exert a powerful impact on school culture and on student learning.

There are a number of effective co-teaching models, including the following:

- **Two or more teachers in the classroom share the instructional tasks.** One teacher might lead a brief mini-lesson while the other develops a concept map of the content on the board or on chart paper. As students work in small groups, one teacher might provide direct instruction to students who need extra support while the other circulates and interacts with the other groups.
- **Two or more teachers teach subgroups of a larger class.** This is a variation on the first arrangement. It differs in that the teachers plan together and they may bring the students together for large group activities such as presentations or demonstrations, but each teacher assumes responsibility for a different group of students.

- **Team members plan together but each member teaches specialized skills to the whole group.** This model is sometimes used when several classes of students are taking the same subject and teachers can take advantage of their areas of expertise by having each one teach a portion of the curriculum to all the classes. Note, however, that this model can lead to a fragmented curriculum and discontinuity for the students if teachers do not plan carefully and communicate well with each other. When teachers work across disciplines, this kind of teaming can highlight for students the interrelationships between subjects, for example, math and science or social studies and English language arts.

Co-teaching requires teachers to relinquish sole ownership of their classrooms, to share responsibility for students, and to change their teaching practices. Teachers who would like to work together need to discuss and make decisions about teaching philosophy and style; working relationships; curriculum, instruction, and assessment; classroom organization and management; the physical environment; communication with administration and parents/guardians; and relationships with students. The blackline master "Planning for Co-teaching: Questions to Consider" included at the back of this book provides a framework for working through the discussion and decision making required for effective co-teaching.

Classroom Inquiry and Action Research

Many of the questions that arise as professional learning communities explore topics of interest can become the focus for classroom inquiry/action research. This process—as shown in the graphic below—involves continually gathering data related to an inquiry question; analyzing, discussing, and writing about the data; taking action; assessing results; developing new questions; and beginning

Action Research

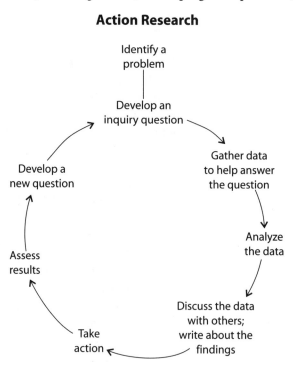

Ideally, the action research process results in the discovery of new information about improving learning conditions. Once the new information is acquired the action researcher makes decisions about how to change practices to include this new learning—or whether to launch additional investigation.
Brighton, 2009, p. 44

the process again. This type of critical inquiry can greatly enhance efforts to improve student learning. The sharing of discoveries and questions related to an ongoing classroom inquiry can lead to extremely dynamic and purposeful professional learning community meetings.

What Is Action Research?

Engaging in action research involves taking something teachers do all the time in an informal way—gathering information on their practices—and making it more formal and public. Inquiry questions arise from teachers' reflections on how well their students are progressing. When teachers identify aspects of student learning that puzzle or trouble them, they can use action research to find out more about the problem and explore solutions. Powerful inquiry questions relate directly to the issue or problem that is causing concern. Questions need to be answerable, however—that is, they can be investigated by accessing information readily available to teachers.

In order to construct answerable questions, teachers might begin by brainstorming the larger problem in the form of questions. Rule out questions that can be answered by "yes" or "no"; instead, formulate questions that begin with "why," "how," or "what." When designing action research, plan to collect different kinds of data. Multiple sources of information will strengthen the validity of the findings. When you are no longer learning anything new from the information you are collecting, you can begin to analyze it. A practical way to begin is to sort the data into piles that constitute categories or themes. Talking and writing about what the data reveal is a way of clarifying what you have learned and of generating new questions.

A professional learning community interested in designing such an inquiry approach can adapt the following process. (Note that before developing an action research project, the group may wish to become better informed about this form of inquiry through professional reading or viewing. See the resources suggested on page 114 at the back of this book.)

1. Develop a question that can be investigated in the group members' classrooms. For example, a professional learning community that has concerns about student problem solving in math might focus their inquiry through a question such as, "In what ways and in what contexts are students applying the problem-solving strategies that they have been taught?"

2. Determine what data will be collected and in what time frame. The types of data can include:
   - Teacher observations recorded through written notes, audiotapes, or videotapes
   - Student journals or learning logs
   - Other student work (assignments or projects)
   - Responses to classroom assessments, including student self-assessments
   - Information from district, provincial/state, or national assessments
   - Student interviews

- Student/teacher conferences
- Observations of peer conferences

3. Analyze the data as individuals and as a group. Teachers can begin by examining the data from their own classrooms and then bring both the data and their initial analyses to the next professional learning community meeting. The group can look for patterns and generate further questions for additional data gathering. Or, they may decide to take action, for example, by reteaching concepts that are unclear to students, and then collect more data. This process can be repeated as many times as is helpful.

4. As the inquiry continues, the group may decide to expand their knowledge through further reading or by contacting someone with expertise related to the question they are investigating. For example, they could contact another teacher or an administrator in their school or in a neighboring school, a curriculum consultant, or a university faculty member.

5. At some point, the group may find it helpful to share their findings with other teachers in the school or with the administration in order to broaden the discussion. Such consultation can lead to the generation of further questions that begin the cycle anew.

Web 2.0 —Enhancing Action Research Through Technology

A professional learning community engaged in action research might be able to involve individuals with outside expertise in their inquiries by connecting with university faculty members online. University/school collaborative action research projects supported by technology can help to build research capabilities among teachers through the input of experienced scholarly researchers. Furthermore, academics have the benefit of ongoing interaction with experts in a particular field.

Teachers can share notes and reflections related to ongoing classroom inquiries through blogs. Narratives and reports related to teacher action research can be posted on the school or district website or submitted to online teacher networks (as described in Chapter 1) or to professional journals. Online tools may also be helpful *within* a school, sustaining long-term collaboration when frequent face-to-face meetings are difficult to arrange. Teachers can share reflections, questions, and insights through online discussion groups, blogs, or something as simple as an email listserve.

Sharing the Teaching Load

When teachers contemplate moving from their customary, and often comfortable, individual work patterns toward collaborative teaching, they often express concerns about having to spend more time in planning and preparation as a result of working with peers compared to when they worked in isolation. In reality, there are always challenges in finding time to meet on a regular basis. Also, as teachers learn to work together, there can be growing pains related to reconciling different perspectives and teaching styles. With experience, however, collaborative work groups can become very efficient in how they use time and in how creatively they channel their diverse knowledge, skills, and interests to the benefit of everyone. Collaboration can result in a lightening of the teaching load for individual teachers as they share responsibilities across the group. Moreover, the energy, enthusiasm, and synergy that result from collective efforts can help teachers remain engaged and excited about teaching.

Chapter 7 describes several different scenarios highlighting the diverse ways in which learning evolves within professional learning communities. The teachers in these scenarios demonstrated a high degree of self-direction, commitment to learning together, and openness to exploring alternative paths. The examples provide models for how professional learning communities can engage in continuous learning that is supported by trust among colleagues.

CHAPTER 7

No Beginning, No End

When we work for the common good, we experience each other in new ways. We don't worry about differences, or status, or traditional relationships. We worry about whether we'll succeed in accomplishing what needs to be done. We focus on the work, not on each other. We learn what trust is. We learn the necessity of good communications.
Wheatley, 2002, p. 126

The learning within a dynamic and productive professional learning community reflects the diverse, ever-changing school contexts in which teachers perform their roles. There is no one right way to construct and sustain professional learning. Although each of the chapters in this book highlights a particular type of activity related to building a professional learning community, all of these activities are interconnected and mutually supportive. Once a professional learning community is up and running, the focus of the collaborative work evolves in response to the insights and questions that arise from within the group, but it also takes shape as the result of externally generated mandates.

Professional Learning Communities in Action

The following scenarios are just a few examples of how a professional learning community might draw upon the activities described in this book in different sequences and combinations. Each of the scenarios demonstrates a different starting place and a different evolution of the collaborative endeavors.

Improving Writing Workshops

The ten teachers of Grades 1 to 3 in Springview Elementary School had two hours of professional learning community meeting time scheduled each week. The teachers had been trying to establish writing workshops with their students, but a number of them were struggling with how to organize their classrooms, moving from a teacher-centred program based on writing prompts to a program in which students choose their own topics. Each teacher had done some professional reading and had attended workshops on how to teach writing, but changing their practices was proving to be difficult. Teachers brought their questions and frustrations to the professional learning community meeting and decided to focus their work on how to plan, organize, and carry out a writing workshop with young children. Although they could have started with more professional reading, several of the teachers said that they did not need more information; they needed to understand how the writing workshop could function in their classrooms.

The group decided to begin by **examining professional practices** through visits to other classrooms to observe how each teacher was currently handling the workshop. The teachers worked in pairs and each pair wrote questions to guide their observations. The group members completed the observations and then shared what they had learned. They discovered that everyone was having difficulty keeping mini-lessons short and focused. Their mini-lessons typically lasted 30 minutes or more, effectively turning the workshop into teacher-centred instruction. The students had little time to write and they continued to be very dependent on the teachers for direction. Teachers noted that students did not seem to know what to write about when teachers did not provide prompts.

Having identified specific areas of concern, the teachers proceeded as follows:

1. They found relevant **professional reading** and expanded their knowledge of how to conduct effective mini-lessons and pre-writing experiences to help students become more independent writers.
2. They found **video resources on DVD and online** demonstrating how different teachers handle the writing workshop.
3. They **experimented with different practices** and discussed their experiences. They **designed mini-lessons together**; each teacher taught these mini-lessons and then reflected on the results.
4. After implementing new practices, teachers **examined student work** dating from before they made the changes and then after they made the changes, and they analyzed the comparative results.
5. They did more **professional reading** about the development of writing skills in young children and **examined the student work again**, looking for evidence of growth.
6. They carefully **reviewed the outcomes/standards for student achievement** in writing for their grade levels and determined strengths and weaknesses in their students' writing relative to the standards.
7. They made **further changes in practices** based upon what they had learned. They continued to visit other classrooms.

The process continued as new questions arose and teachers became more comfortable with the structure of the writing workshop. They began thinking about how they could foster reading/writing connections and how they could challenge their best writers. They examined the results of external assessments to see how their students compared to the expected outcomes/standards. They continued to seek out new ideas through professional reading and viewing, as well as through interactions with teachers beyond the school through a district-sponsored interactive website.

Improving External Assessment Results

The Jackson Street High School serves a diverse community of working-class families and newly arrived immigrants from around the world. The results of external assessments showed that the majority of students were not meeting expectations. Teachers had adjusted their programs to respond to the large number of English language learners and other students with histories of poor school achievement. The district had appointed a new principal with the directive to make improvement of external assessment results a priority.

Late in the school year before the principal took over, the district provided two professional development days for the staff and access to district consultants for a session related to **analyzing the results of the external assessments**. Over the summer, the principal devised a schedule that provided common release time for small groups of teachers to work in professional learning communities. The principal set broad parameters for the work of these small groups: each group must take action to improve student learning, using the analysis of external assessments as a starting point. The school's professional development days were intended to share the ongoing work of the small groups.

The science teachers formed a cross-grade grouping and began by discussing the implications of the analysis of external assessments for their subject area. Although external testing was not done in science, the teachers could see that the large number of students struggling with literacy and numeracy contributed to poor performance in science, as documented through classroom assessments. They began their work by **examining outcomes/standards** in their own area, but also in English language arts and math as well to develop a better understanding of what was expected in terms of student learning in each area of the curriculum. They asked the principal for the opportunity to use a professional development day to **meet in cross-disciplinary groups** to talk with teachers in other subject areas about their insights. As a result of the professional development session, all of the subject area professional learning communities made a commitment to focus on literacy and numeracy.

The science teachers decided to begin by **examining student work** from their classrooms, each choosing a number of examples representing different levels of student performance. The group discussed the strengths and weaknesses evident in the work and considered the students' responses in relationship to outcomes/standards. They noted that a subset of students was struggling with the mathematical aspects of chemistry and physics. Many more students—almost all of them, in fact—were having difficulty coping with reading textbooks and with writing up labs, reports, and projects. In truth, the teachers felt rather overwhelmed by the problems that they had uncovered.

The chemistry and physics teachers volunteered to meet with the math teachers to discuss how they might **plan in cross-disciplinary teams** to address the areas of weakness that were impacting performance in science. The school's resource teacher took part in these discussions and agreed to work with a small group of particularly needy students. The math teachers used the insights from their discussions with the science teachers as part of their focus on students' independent application of math concepts and skills.

The science teachers decided that they needed to learn more about reading and writing in science, so they found relevant **professional readings** and examined **online resources.** They also looked for practical information on working with English language learners in high school content area classrooms. They realized that the approaches suggested for students learning English would also support other students struggling with literacy.

The teachers agreed that it would be helpful for them to **jointly plan** and then teach a unit in which they incorporated their new insights into how to support students. As part of that planning, they **developed common assessments**. As they were developing the plan, they consulted with the school's resource teacher, support teachers for English language learners, and the district's science consultant. The latter was enrolled in a master's program at the local university and put them in touch with a professor who had expertise in literacy and science. The professor participated in their group both on-site and through **videoconferencing**.

The teachers implemented the unit and examined the results of the common assessments. The students in one of the classrooms outperformed all of the others. In teaching the unit, that teacher had used small group work more extensively and had incorporated more concrete and visual models. She had also chosen to **team teach** with the resource teacher. Her colleagues had been less willing to transform their practices, and the differences showed up in the results of the assessments. The group engaged in honest discussions about the differences in practice and decided to engage in more intense **lesson study** in which they would design a lesson together and then observe it being taught by the teacher with the impressive assessment results. The teachers continued to expand their knowledge of effective teaching practices, develop curriculum together, and examine assessment results openly and critically.

Dealing with Externally Initiated Curriculum Change

The social studies teachers from Prince Street Middle School were not happy. They had just attended a two-day district-level professional development session where a new social studies curriculum for Grades 6 to 8 had been introduced. The seven teachers had been members of a school-based professional learning community for more than a year and they had been working together to enhance students' critical thinking. Now, the principal had passed along a district directive requiring the group to shift their attention to the new curriculum to prepare for implementation the following fall.

Resigned to giving up their self-selected inquiry, the teachers decided that they really needed to gain a better understanding of the changes in the curriculum. They had received new curriculum documents as well as new teaching resources. They used a **jigsaw reading/discussion model**, to **examine the new materials**. They were pleased to discover that critical thinking received a major emphasis in the new curriculum and they congratulated themselves on their foresight! Feeling more positive about the curriculum change, the teachers became more enthusiastic about working through it together. Their discussion focused on how they could build upon the work that they had been doing around critical thinking.

The teachers' examination of the materials also revealed that there was much more multicultural content in the program as well as the use of multiple resources rather than a single textbook. The teachers determined that they needed to engage in a program of **professional reading** to enhance their knowledge of multiculturalism. They spent several months working with the new materials, reading book chapters and articles, and tapping into online resources. They located a social studies teachers' **online network** that connected them with teachers in other provinces and states. They also continued to share insights into their ongoing work centred on critical thinking.

As the year progressed, the teachers decided to **joint-plan** one short unit from the new curriculum and to try it out in their classrooms. They designed and taught this unit and discussed the results. For the rest of that year and during the following two years, the teachers

1. **jointly developed** and continued to revise a curriculum plan for the year
2. worked with the principal to develop a schedule that provided opportunities for them to **observe lessons being taught in each other's classrooms** and to **team teach**
3. joined a province-wide **online network** of teachers implementing the new curriculum

4. chose particular assignments and brought in **samples of student work to examine**
5. considered the samples in relationship to **provincial outcomes/standards**
6. decided they needed to expand their repertoire of classroom assessment practices, so they did additional **professional reading** and then developed **common assessments**
7. examined the results of assessments and continued to **change teaching practices.**

At the end of the second year of implementation, the teachers felt comfortable with the new curriculum and they were very pleased with the multicultural emphasis. They decided to meet with the English language arts teachers to explore possibilities for **cross-disciplinary joint planning** that could further extend students' cross-cultural awareness through both programs. This led to a whole-school focus on multiculturalism supported by teachers working across disciplines.

Implementing a School- or District-Wide Mandate

The Washington County School District prided itself on its commitment to student learning. The senior staff shared a belief in the need for a coherent, district-wide approach to improvement. As part of their reform agenda, the district mandated that all schools establish professional learning communities and that all of these groups focus on the development of common assessments.

The principal of Meadowbrook High School, a rural Grades 7 to 12 secondary school, knew that she was obligated to carry out this mandate, but she was concerned about how the teachers would interpret it. The staff had tried to develop common exams in the past but the process had proved to be very contentious. Teachers held strong, contrasting beliefs about what and how to teach, despite the existence of a curriculum that included explicit student achievement outcomes/standards.

The principal decided that she would need to take a leadership role in interpreting the mandate within her school. She had already initiated the idea of collaborative work through well-established grade-level and subject-area groupings. These groups had been working on aspects of the school-improvement plan for over two years. There was a subject-area teacher leader structure in place, so the principal engaged the teacher leaders in professional development related to examining the curriculum expectations and classroom assessment. She asked these leaders to guide the subject-area professional learning communities through a process of **deconstructing outcomes/standards** as well as **learning more about formative classroom assessment** in each subject area.

The subject-area professional learning communities spent an entire year engaged in these two activities prior to beginning to draft common assessments. Each of the groups developed its own process, but at some time during the year they all

- engaged in **professional reading** related to classroom assessment
- **deconstructed the outcomes/standards** in their subject area
- shared **examples of current assessments and student responses** to those assessments

- **jointly planned lessons** designed to support specific outcomes, taught the lessons, and reflected on their experiences
- tried out new forms of assessment in their classrooms and **observed each other's practices**

During the second year, the teachers began to design and implement common assessments in each subject area. Because of their year's work together, they had developed a much more consistent and coherent shared understanding of the curricular expectations and of ways to assess students' progress toward achieving outcomes. They had also identified areas of the curriculum that needed more attention in their classrooms.

The teacher leaders continued to meet regularly with the principal, sharing their experiences and supporting each others' leadership work. As questions arose within this group, the principal provided them with additional professional development opportunities. They became a dynamic professional learning community of teacher leaders that helped to move the school toward a student-focused, coherent approach to learning for both teachers and students.

Sustaining the Learning

Professional learning communities exert their efforts slowly, yet sustainably, over time. Their success depends on continuing support from outside the school, compatibility with external reform imperatives, strong support in terms of instructional materials and leadership development, and a staff with sufficient levels of knowledge, competence, and skill to share with their colleagues.
Hargreaves, 2003, p. 172

Although the situations described in these scenarios involve a range of different contexts and reasons for professional learning communities to work together, the collaborations shared a number of commonalities that contributed to their long-term success:

- Strong leadership demonstrated by the school administrator and by the teacher leaders within the small groups
- Responsiveness to changing needs and to new questions that arose
- Variety and flexibility in terms of activities, groupings, and focus
- Time and freedom to self-direct the content and the pace of collaborative work
- Commitment to changing practices to improve student outcomes
- Patience, open-mindedness, and humor

Throughout this book we have offered practical means through which teachers can engage in collaborative learning. We know that the teachers and administrators who read our book will develop many interesting variations and extensions of our ideas. They will also invent their own ways of working together, bringing their professional knowledge and experience to the process. In the professional learning communities in which we have been involved, we have experienced a great deal of learning, thoughtful conversation, critical reflection, and laughter. We have also witnessed the ways in which the members of collaborative groups support each other, no matter whether everything is going well or whether things seem to be falling apart. In both situations, it is better to be part of a community than to go it alone.

The journey from a culture of isolation and individuality to one in which collaboration is valued as the best means to improve student learning is complex and often rocky. We hope that the activities and suggestions that we have shared in this book will help to ease the way for the many principals and teachers striving to make professional learning communities a reality in their schools.

Blackline Masters

Principal's Communication Form: Professional Learning Communities

This form is intended to keep me informed regarding the work of the professional learning communities in the school so that I can support them in every way possible. I will return this form to you with my comments before your next meeting. Please fill in and submit this form each month, updating it from the previous report as your learning evolves. Good luck!

Date: _____

Group members: _____

Learning focus (please indicate if, and if so, how this focus has changed since your last report):

_____

_____

_____

Meetings and activities this month:

_____

_____

_____

_____

Highlight important insights or questions that have emerged:

• _____

_____

• _____

_____

How can I support your work?

_____

_____

Principal's feedback:

_____

_____

_____

Literature Circle Roles for Teacher Discussion Groups

Connector

Your job is to make connections. As you read, focus on how the book or article relates to your own teaching experiences, to some aspect of your school or community, to something you heard about in the news, to something you read about elsewhere or learned in a course—or make any other connection that occurs to you. The book may remind you of another book that you read on the topic or another book by the same author. The content may be consistent with what you know or it may offer new ideas for consideration. For example: Some connections I made to my own teaching experiences, to other reading, or to what I know about the topic are….

Questioner

Your job is to write down questions that arise from your reading. Was there anything you didn't understand? As you read, what did you wonder about? Did anything about the text confuse you? Did you have questions about unfamiliar concepts that the author discussed? Was there unfamiliar vocabulary? Did you have questions about the relevance of the content of the text to your class-room and the school? Did questions arise that might lead to further reading or research to gather more information?

   As you read or after you finish reading, think about what you asked yourself along the way. Write down these questions to share with the group. For example: How might I adapt the ideas the author suggested for working with older elementary students to suit my Grade 2 class?

Literary Luminary/Passage Master

Your job is to record sections of texts or direct quotations for the group to discuss. These should be selections that are particularly powerful, well-written, relevant, puzzling, or provocative—in short, examples of the author's writing that are worth further thought and discussion. When you record the passage, make note of why you chose it. Decide how you will share the selected text: read it aloud yourself, have someone else read it aloud, or read silently and then discuss it with the group.

Illustrator

Here is an opportunity to represent your responses through images rather than words. While good readers use visualization when reading fiction, visualization is also a way of understanding informa-tional text in a different way. As you read, be conscious of the pictures that you are forming in your mind: Do you imagine the classroom or the student the author is writing about? Do you visualize one of your learners or your own classroom? Does the text evoke other kinds of images, perhaps from nature or the media? The mental image can represent something directly from the text or it can convey your feelings about the text or your reaction to the author's stance. As your response, draw or represent in a visual way (e.g. by means of a collage) something related to the text. Don't worry if you can't draw well. Create stick figures, make a simple sketch, draw a diagram or flowchart, or use paint or other art materials to create an abstract image. Use words for labels if that is helpful.

Interpreting Outcomes/Standards

What the Outcome/Standard Says	What the Outcome/Standard Means for "Me/Us" in Terms of the Classroom, Grade Level, and School	Questions/Concerns

Deconstructing Outcomes into Classroom-Level Achievement/Learning Targets

Outcomes	Outcome(s) Translated into Classroom-Level Learning Targets	Outcomes Translated into Student-Friendly Language (Statements my students will be able to make at the end of the unit)
	Knowledge/Understanding	
	Reasoning	
	Skills	
	Products	
	Dispositions	

Evidence of Meeting the Outcome(s)/Targets

I will know that students have met the outcome(s)/targets if they:

Opportunities for Assessment

Students will be able to demonstrate their understanding through:

Questions to Guide Examination of Student Work

Adapted from a framework developed by the Looking at Student Work Association (www.lasw.org)

Focusing Questions

- How well does this project meet the criteria for the assignment?

- Based on the students' responses, how appropriate was this assignment for these learners? What could be done to make it more appropriate?

- What evidence is there in these samples that students understand key concepts or skills?

- How can I encourage students to take more risks?

- What evidence is there that students found this task engaging? What was each student trying to do?

Clarifying Questions

- How many days did the students have to work on this project?

- Did the students work independently or in groups?

- What experiences did the students have before beginning this project/task?

Probing Questions

- Why did you structure the assignment this way?

- What would happen if you changed the group members?

- Have you experienced anything like this before?

- What do you think would have to change for the students to take more responsibility for their own learning?

Reflective Questions

- What went well in this session?

- What did we learn? What insights into our inquiry question did the session contribute?

- Are we getting better at asking probing questions?

- How might we improve the process?

Can-Do Writing Assessment Form

Student's Name: _____ Age: _____ Grade: _____

Date of Sample: _____ Teacher: _____

Context of the Writing Activity:

Format: _____ Audience: _____

_____

_____

_____

Evidence of What the Writer CAN DO:

_____

_____

_____

_____

_____

_____

_____

_____

_____

_____

_____

Number of running words used: _____ Spelling accuracy (%): _____

Evaluator: _____ Date: _____

What Makes a Good Lesson Plan?

- In what ways and to what extent does the lesson plan contribute to each student's growth toward achieving the outcomes/standards of the curriculum in our school?

- Is the methodology sound, based on our understanding of preferred practices in the curriculum for which the lesson is intended?

- Are the purposes and intended achievement target(s) of the lesson clearly stated?

- To what extent and in what ways do the learning experiences within the lesson fulfill the stated purposes and contribute to students' growth as learners?

- Are suggestions for assessment for learning included as an integral part of the learning experiences?

- Is the lesson clearly and logically organized? Is it well sequenced so that the suggested activities/learning experiences are well connected and flow smoothly? Is the lesson sufficiently flexible so that it could be adapted as needed? Are approximate time frames noted?

- Does the lesson clearly outline what the teacher and the students will be doing throughout the lesson? Is there a balance between teacher instruction and student small group and independent learning?

- Is the lesson appropriate for my/our learners?
    - Will it be of interest to them?
    - Does it have the potential to engage them?
    - Do the students have the necessary background knowledge and experiences to take advantage of this lesson? How will it extend their understandings?
    - How could I/we modify the lesson to make it more responsive to the needs of our students?

- Would I find this lesson engaging to teach?

- Are the materials that are required readily available in my/our school?

Cross-Disciplinary Planning

Topic or Large Inquiry Question: _____

Subquestions or Subcategories	English Language Arts	Social Studies	Math	Science	Art

Planning for Co-teaching: Questions to Consider

Questions	Notes
Teaching Philosophy and Style • How does each one of us view our roles as teachers? • What does each of us believe about learning? • What strengths does each of us bring? What would each of us like to do better? • What does each of us like best about teaching? What is most frustrating or difficult? • How does each of us prefer to plan? **Working Relationships** • What out-of-school factors (e.g., child care, course work, other family issues, etc.) might influence schedules? • What commitment to work outside of school hours will we make? • What do we have in common? How do we differ from each other? • How often and when will we meet to plan? • How will we resolve differences of opinion? **Curriculum, Instruction, and Assessment** • What format for curricular planning will we use? • What teaching strategies will we use? • What will each of us teach? What will we do jointly? • What resources will we use? • What forms of assessment will we use? • How will we keep records of students' progress?	

Planning for Co-teaching: Questions to Consider *continued*

Questions	Notes
Classroom Organization and Management • What types of grouping will we use? • What rules/expectations can we agree upon? • What classroom routines will we establish? • How much freedom will students have to move around the room? • How much noise can each of us tolerate? • How will we handle student discipline? **Physical Environment** • How will we arrange furniture (storage units, student tables/desks, teacher's desk)? • How will we organize materials (teacher resources, student resources, supplies)? • Which materials does each of us own? What will we share? **Communication** • How will we handle communication with parents/guardians? • Will we hold individual or joint parent conferences? • How and how often will we interact with school administrators? **Interaction With Students** • What will be our shared norms for interacting with students? • Which student-related responsibilities will we assign to one person; which responsibilities will we share?	

Bibliography

Brighton, C. (2009). "Embarking on Action Research." *Educational Leadership*, 66(5), 40–44.

Bunting, C. (2009). "Come, Listen and Learn." *Phi Delta Kappan*, 90(7), 518–520.

Clarke, Shirley. (2005). *Formative Assessment in Action: Weaving the Elements Together.* London: Hodder Murray.

Church, S. M., J. Baskwill, and M. Swain. (2007) *Yes, but…if they like it, they'll learn it!* Markham, ON: Pembroke.

Daniels, H. (2002). *Literature Circles.* Portland, ME: Stenhouse.

Darling-Hammond, L., and N. Richardson (2009). "Teacher Learning: What Matters?" *Educational Leadership*, 66(5), 46–53.

DuFour, R. (2004). "Schools as Learning Communities." *Educational Leadership*, 61(8), 6–11.

Ferriter, B. (2009). "Learning with Blogs and Wikis." *Educational Leadership*, 66(5), 34–38.

Hargreaves, A. (2003). *Teaching in the Knowledge Society.* New York: Teachers College Press.

Harvey, S., and A. Goudvis. (2007). *Strategies That Work* (2nd edition). Portland, ME: Stenhouse.

Harste, J. C., K. G. Short, with C. Burke (1988). *Creating Classrooms for Authors.* Portsmouth, NH: Heinemann.

Hunt, R. "What is Inkshedding?" Retrieved July 8, 2009 from the following website: www.stthomasu.ca/~hunt/dialogic/whatshed.htm

Jacobs, H. (2004). "Development of a Consensus Map." In H. Jacobs (ed). *Getting Results With Curriculum Mapping.* Alexandria, VA: Association for Supervision and Curriculum Development, 25–35.

Knobel, M., and D. Wilber. (2009). "Let's Talk 2.0." *Educational Leadership*, 66(6), 20–24.

Manitoba Education, Citizenship and Youth. *Curriculum Frameworks of Outcomes.* Retrieved June 23, 2009 from the following website: www.edu.gov.mb.ca/ks4/cur/types.html

Marzano, R. J. (2003). *What Works in Schools.* Alexandria, VA: Association for Supervision and Curriculum Development.

Meier, D. (2002). *In Schools We Trust.* Boston: Beacon Press.

National Council of Teachers of English. (1995). "Position Statement on Interdisciplinary Learning, Pre-K to Grade 4." Retrieved June 30, 2009 from the following website (enter title of article into "Search" box): www.ncte.org/positions/statements/interdisclearnprek4

Reeves, D. (2009). "Three Challenges of Web 2.0." *Educational Leadership*, 66(6), 87–89.

Schmoker, M. (2004). "Tipping Point: From Feckless Reform to Substantive Instructional Improvement. *Phi Delta Kappan*, 85(6), 425–432.

Schmoker, M. (2006). *Results Now*. Alexandria, VA: Association for Supervision and Curriculum Development.

Southwest Educational Development Laboratory. "Professional Learning Communities: What Are They and Why Are They Important?" Retrieved April 15, 2009 from the following website: www.sedl.org/change/issues/issues61.html

Spence, C. (2009). *Leading With Passion and Purpose*. Markham, ON: Pembroke.

Stiggins, R. J., J. A. Arter, J. Chappuis, and S. Chappuis. (2004). *Classroom Assessment for Student Learning: Doing It Right—Using It Well*. Portland, OR: Assessment Training Institute.

Stiggins, R. (2008). *An Introduction to Student-Involved Assessment for Learning* (5th edition). Upper Saddle River, N.J.: Pearson Education.

Stiggins, R., and R. DuFour. (2009). "Maximizing the Power of Formative Assessments." *Phi Delta Kappan*, 90(9), 640–644.

Watanabe, T. (2002). "Learning From Japanese Lesson Study." *Educational Leadership*, 59(60), 36–39.

Wheatley, M. (2002). *Turning to One Another: Simple Conversations to Restore Hope to the Future*. San Francisco, CA: Berrett-Koehler.

Wiggins, G. P., and J. McTighe. (2005). *Understanding by Design*. Alexandria, VA: Association for Supervision and Curriculum Development.

Wyche-Smith, S. "Everything You Wanted to Know About Your Students' Responses to Class, But Were Afraid to Ask Inkshedding." Retrieved April 15, 2009 from the following website:

www.evergreen.edu/washcenter/resources/acl/c3.html

Recommended Resources

Logistics and Leadership

Allen, J. (2006). *Becoming a Literacy Leader*. Portland, ME: Stenhouse.

Allen, J. (2008). *Teacher Study Groups*. DVD (22 minutes) plus study guide. Portland, ME: Stenhouse.

Church, S. (2005). *The Principal Difference*. Markham, ON: Pembroke.

DuFour, R., R. DuFour, R. Eaker, and G. Karhanek. (2004). *Whatever It Takes— How Professional Learning Communities Respond When Kids Don't Learn*. Bloomington, IN: National Education Service.

DuFour, R., R. Eaker, and R. DuFour. (2006). *Learning by Doing: A Handbook for Professional Learning Communities at Work*. Mission, BC: Solution Tree, Canada.

Easton, L. (2009). *Protocols for Professional Learning Communities*. Alexandria, VA: Association for Supervision and Curriculum Development.

Foster, G. (2008). *Working Together to Improve Literacy*. Markham, ON: Pembroke.

Hord, S. (2008). *Leading Professional Learning Communities*. Thousand Oaks, CA: Corwin.

Niday, D., J. Potts, M. Johnson, and J. Boreen (2009). *Mentoring Beginning Teachers* (2nd edition). Portland, ME: Stenhouse.

Wenger, E., R. McDermott, and W. Snyder. (2002). *Cultivating Communities of Practice*. Cambridge, MA: Harvard Business School Press.

Web 2.0

Cole, C., K. Ray, and J. Zanetis. (2009). *Videoconferencing for K–12 Classrooms* (2nd edition). Eugene, OR: International Society for Technology in Education.

Schrum, L., and G. Solomon. (2007). *Web 2.0: New Tools, New Schools*. Eugene, OR: International Society for Technology in Education.

Video Resources from Teachers TV. Retrieved May 15, 2009 from the following website: www. teachers.tv/video/4883

Assessment

Black, P., C. Harrison., C. Lee, B. Marshall, and D. William. (2003). *Assessment for Learning: Putting It into Practice*. Berkshire, England: Open University Press, McGraw-Hill Education.

Davies, A. (2007). *Making Classroom Assessment Work* (2nd edition). Courtney, B.C.: Connections Publishing.

Gregory, K., C. Cameron, and A. Davies. (1997). *Setting and Using Criteria.* Courtney, B.C.: Connections Publishing.

Gregory, K., C. Cameron, and A. Davies. (2000). *Self-Assessment and Goal Setting.* Courtney, B.C.: Connections Publishing.

Gregory, K., C. Cameron, and A. Davies. (2001). *Conferencing and Reporting.* Courtney, B.C.: Connections Publishing.

O'Connor, K. (2002). *How to Grade for Learning* (2nd edition). Thousand Oaks, CA: Corwin.

Examining Student Work/Lesson Study

Lesson Study Research Group www.tc.edu/centers/lessonstudy

Looking at Student Work Association www.lasw.org

National School Reform Faculty www.nsrfharmony.org

Stepanik, J., G. Appel, M. Leong, M. T. Manga, and M. Mitchell. (2007). *Leading Lesson Study: A Practical Guide for Teachers and Facilitators.* Thousand Oaks, CA: Corwin Press.

Interdisciplinary Teaching

Edutopia. "What Is Integrated Studies?" Retrieved July 9, 2009 from the following website: www.edutopia.org/integrated-studies

Jacobs, H. H. (ed.). (2004). *Getting Results With Curriculum Mapping.* Alexandria, VA: Association for Supervision and Curriculum Development.

Action Research

George Mason University Graduate School of Education. "What Is Action Research?" Retrieved May 3, 2009 from the following website: www.gse.gmu.edu/research/tr/tr_action/

Hendricks, C. C. (2008). *Improving Schools Through Action Research: A Comprehensive Guide for Educators.* Needham Heights, MA: Allyn and Bacon, a division of Pearson.

Johnson, A. P. (2008). *Action Research.* Needham Heights, MA: Allyn and Bacon, a division of Pearson.

The Northeast Florida Science, Technology, and Mathematics Center for Education. "Action Research for Teachers." Retrieved May 3, 2009 from the following website: www.nefstem.org/teacher_guide/intro/index.htm

Index